MYSTICS,
MAGICIANS,
AND
MEDICINE
PEOPLE

AN OMEGA BOOK

This New Age series of Paragon House is dedicated to classic and contemporary works about higher human development and the nature of ultimate reality. *Omega Books* encompasses the fields of mysticism and spirituality, psychic research and paranormal phenomena, the evolution of consciousness, and the human potential for self-directed growth in body, mind, and spirit.

MYSTICS, MAGICIANS, AND MEDICINE PEOPLE

TALES OF A WANDERER

Doug Boyd

PARAGON HOUSE
New York

First paperback edition 1991
Published in the United States by
Paragon House
90 Fifth Avenue
New York, NY 10011

Designed by Deirdre C. Amthor
Manufactured in the United States of America

Library of Congress Cataloging in Publication Data
Boyd, Doug.
  Mystics, magicians, and medicine people: tales of a wanderer
  Doug Boyd.—1st ed.
     p. cm.
  ISBN 1-55778-127-3: $10.95
     1. Boyd, Doug. 2. Religion—United States—
  Biography. 3. New Age movement. I. Title.
  BL73.B68A3   1989
  291—dc20   89-32813
  ISBN 1-55778-463-9   CIP

The paper used in this publication meets the minimum
requirements of American National Standard for Information
Sciences—Permanence of Paper for Printed Library Materials,
ANSI Z39.48-1984.

This book is dedicated to the most constant and caring of all my teachers—my own parents, Alyce and Elmer Green.

CONTENTS

ACKNOWLEDGMENTS   ix

PROLOGUE   God's Feet   xi

SCENE ONE   The Farmer's Mind Field   1

SCENE TWO   No Shame—No Blame   19

SCENE THREE   Do Not Get Hit   41

SCENE FOUR   The Soft Body   62

SCENE FIVE   Ask and You Shall Be Pushed   80

SCENE SIX   The Monk From the Past   104

SCENE SEVEN   Henry and Joseph Himself   127

SCENE EIGHT   The Story Continues   161

ACKNOWLEDGMENTS

I must first express my gratitude for the invaluable editorial and conceptual assistance provided by David Bane during the preparation of this manuscript. Then I must acknowledge the many friends, colleagues, and coworkers who have been helpful and supportive over the years: Hugh and Ruth Harrison of the Esmeralda-Continuum Foundation, Miriam Camp of Berkeley, Jack Schwarz of the Aletheia Foundation, my colleagues of the Cross-Cultural Studies Program and of the International Center for Integrative Studies, and Will Noffke of Shared Visions in Berkeley, to name a few. Finally, I am grateful to all of those, named and unnamed, who are part of this story.

PROLOGUE

God's Feet

If I have learned one thing in this life, it is that God will not tie my shoes without me.

At age four, we are supposed to be able to tie our own shoes. This was the case when I was four at any rate, because all little children's shoes had laces. I knew how, but I supposed myself to be much less adept than I really was. I was one of those kids who at age four (and there may be many, many more than we realize or admit) still clearly remembered and quite regularly reflected upon that realm whence I had so recently come; and this practice was particularly attractive to me when faced with such worldly nuisances as putting on my shoes. It could take me hours to get dressed—and it frequently did! My parents and other family members realized that if they kept coming to my aid, I would never learn. But then, they also realized that if they kept waiting patiently for me, I would not learn either.

So, for reasons that seemed to me quite beyond my control, frequent scoldings began to fall upon my little ears as I sat with my chin on my knee and my shoelaces in my fingers, seemingly daydreaming, gazing intermittently at my shoes, and drifting in and out of focus. One Sunday morning as I was about to make us all late for church, I sat helplessly on the floor, knowing that none of my family was willing to assist me. Apparently, it occurred to me on that day that God was always there to help. After all, I was trying to make it to Sunday school. My parents heard me through the open doorway as I called out. They peered through the door to watch from behind my back—and I came to be reminded of that day several times as I grew older.

"God!" I repeated over and over, looking first at the ceiling and then at my feet. "God! Tie my shoes!" It went on for some time. "God, can't you hear me? I said for you to tie my shoes!" Nothing happened, and I fell silent for a long moment. No doubt I had somehow to deal with this apparent rejection. "Well," I said at last, quietly pondering aloud to myself, "I'm part of God." And then, in a high, cheerful voice, as though I had just felt for the first time the thrill of that reality: "So I'll tie them myself!"

That little bit of perennial wisdom, voiced as it was from my tiny head, amused my parents and then their friends at church. But, of course, it was not my wisdom. I had simply learned it at that very Sunday school. "I am part of God, I am part of God." We children had all repeated it again and again every Sunday morning. "God is Love, God is Love, and I am part of God." Nothing had been mentioned regarding the tying of shoes; but, as a little kid, I had to experiment somewhat to figure out the implications.

By now I have learned, through my growing years of experimentation and observation, a great deal about those implications. Also, by now, I have gone through many pairs of footwear, with and without laces: sandals, moccasins, wooden clogs, rubber slippers, and leather boots. In my fieldwork and travels, I have observed incidents of prophetic vision. I have watched varieties of traditional healings and invocational rituals. I have seen the honest and purposeful use of true magic. I have witnessed omniscience. Behind the myriad creations of costumes and customs found in all the contrasting cultures lies the same perennial wisdom. I have come to learn of that cosmological arrangement that accounts for the magnificent works and ways of mystics, magicians, and medicine people. I have learned the simple secret of the shaman, the sorcerer, the seer—and I have come to see that it is in fact no secret at all. It is that all things are alive and all life is related.

In my childhood days, I spent many an afternoon and evening on the lap of our family teacher. Though I perhaps could not then grasp the cosmological concepts that came from his lips nor the metaphysical discussions he evoked among my parents and grandparents, I had free and total access to his abundant love and constant cheerfulness. I was the one who shook with his laughter as I sat on his lap.

I received a most delightful lecture from him one day—intended for my own entertainment and education. It was about leprechauns. On and on he went as I bounced on his knee and watched him bob his head and wave his arms through the air—and all I had done was mention the word. I simply wanted to know what it meant, and I inspired the most jubilant and animated expounding I had ever heard from him. "Leprechauns!" he declared. "Most delightful little people! And you want to know all about leprechauns!" His face flushed and his eyes sparkled as he described them for me—from feathered cap to buckled boot. He almost whispered as he told of their benevolent hearts and deeds and their magical powers. And then he chuckled loudly and slapped me on the head and let me in on their wonderful talent for mischief.

"Oh," I said, when at last he had finished, " 'cause Dad told Gramps you're just like a leprechaun." He was. Now I can see it. He was the one who was always talking about God and Divinity, and the whole business felt to me like a tremendous lot of fun. If I had any notion of God at all, it was that since we are all a part of God, God is life—full of play and full of love—and love is absolutely everywhere. I was fortunate. These ideas were endorsed for me again and again throughout my childhood and my ongoing adventures.

My career choice was that of the wanderer. I just wanted to

put on my shoes and go—anywhere. My place, it seemed to me, was wherever I could manage to be. And I managed to be (with the right combination of enticement and resolution) among many different peoples in many places on both sides of the planet and in all corners of my own country. I enjoyed the contrast between what we call the West and the Far East, and I liked seeing the increasing communication among contrasting cultures.

The swamis and babas in India used to challenge me: "For what do you go hither and thither, searching and searching? Why do you search outside yourself? Do you imagine you can find the truth in the farthest corner of the world? You will never be satisfied! Truth is not such a thing that it is far away." But I was not searching outside nor was I seeking satisfaction. I was just wandering. There are the stories of the musk deer who, in search of that wonderful scent of musk that seems always just before them, go on rushing up and down the mountainsides, not realizing that the mysterious smell comes from their very own selves. A deer who does realize this will have peace of mind but will nevertheless, I should hope, go on running here and there just for the joy in it. A deer would never be able to imagine such a devious dichotomy as "inside" and "outside."

Swami Rama, the Himalayan yogi adept with whom I worked in the Voluntary Controls Program at The Menninger Foundation, and about whom I later wrote in my book *Swami,* used to call out again and again—so that the words still ring in my ears: "God is past, present, and future; God is here and there and everywhere, and nothing is outside! Maya does not mean that there is something unreal in this world —maya means to suppose that anything could be unreal. Maya is to look at a tree and think that it is simply a tree. To look at a tree and not see God—this is maya!" The "truly genuine" swamis, he once told me, were perpetual wanderers. "This used to be required," he said. "They never stayed in any one place for more than three days' time. It was not allowed." Even now, there are the sadhus who go here and there from place to place and the Jain monks who softly tread endless miles in their bare feet. Theirs is one way, I once thought to myself, to help the collective creator feel the heartbeat of the Earth. They have no desire to be satisfied. Once when Swami Rama's guru had finished a thoughtful response to a challenging question, he asked the swami— who was then but a young disciple—whether he was satisfied. "Never!" was the confident reply. "I am content, but I am never satisfied!"

Rolling Thunder, the American Indian medicine man about whom I wrote in the book that bears his name, often repeated: "The Great Spirit is right here, right now, all around us. The Great Spirit is in everything you see here—and in a whole lot you may not see, at that. The trees, the birds, everything—this Indian tobacco, even these rocks here—there's no getting away from the Great Spirit." It's true. And true wanderers don't ever wish to get away from anything. By venturing out, they venture in—within this vast, collective "inside" that we are sharing. The life of the wanderer is one of deep contentment. But the wanderer need never be satisfied.

Mad Bear, the Tuscarora medicine man with whom I worked and traveled steadily for more than five years (and about whom I'll share in detail in my next book), often remarked to me: "Our people don't ever say, 'Give us this day,' although I have no disrespect for those who do. Our people do not believe that we are here to ask and receive what we want from the Great Spirit. We are here on this Earth as the very hands and feet of the Great Spirit. We are here to bring about, through our own wits and our own work, what the Great Spirit wants on this Earth." What we are really seeking must be what the Great Spirit wants—that must be what is pulling on us.

Again and again, in sweat lodges, in traditional councils and ceremonies, and even in social gatherings, we hear, "All my relations! All my relations!" Our relations are not limited to family and kinfolk but include all life—and in the sweat lodges, even the rocks are alive. Direct experience and awareness of the interconnectedness of all life will be essential for regaining the natural human potentials that have become so uncommon in modern times. We need a practical and relevant mysticism. Our pressing need to handle our contemporary human emergency now demands of us a better understanding of our relationship to all of life. We cannot honestly address the question, "What in the world is a human being?" except within the context of the larger question, "What in the world is the world?" We cannot know ourselves out of context. No one said, "Know thyself all by thyself." We cannot really understand anything apart from the interconnected cosmic contexture into which it fits. We can never truly understand Earth's Plan, or even life itself, when science and mysticism go on attempting to coexist, in some sort of self-induced schizophrenia, by ignoring each other. We need a practical mysticism—an appropriate balance between intuitive insight and practical effort.

No amount of meditation, chanting, lighting of candles, or burning of incense will induce God or Heaven to tie our shoes for us. There is nothing "outside" to provide for us, to protect us, or to bring us peace. So we'll do it ourselves. Within the contemporary "new consciousness" and "personal growth" movements, there are many who suppose themselves to be much less adept—and much less responsible—than they really are. There are those who, in turning away from the "material" toward the "spiritual," relinquish their handle on earthly affairs and the power of cooperative effort. It becomes expedient to defer to some "upper dimension" to clear up the human condition and let the enlightened humans remain in passive bliss. It's easy to remain blissfully helpless. But we cannot safely sit much longer, waiting for someone or something else to tie our shoes, to provide for our people, to prepare for our peace, to protect our planet. We need to get up and get out, to experience and explore this earthly abode—and, in the process, discover that we are all mystics, magicians, and medicine people.

The scenes that follow are true stories of real people, true events and episodes from my own journals of travels and adventures. I have seldom kept written journals but have always kept mental ones—always kept clear and vivid memories. Over the years, I must have told these stories dozens of times in my trips and talks around the country. In sharing these stories, I believe I'm helping to share a vision—not my vision, exclusively, and not their vision, entirely—but our vision. Somehow, we really must arrive at our collective visions—at the visions we will share.

These stories should be read in sequence so that the reader can follow the references along the path as we go. Along with the stories, I have shared my contemplations and elaborations (in italics), in the hope that you will be moved to come up with your own contemplations—or with your own adventures, actually—and thus your own perspectives. I would be pleased if you would contemplate with me and make your contribution to the enrichment of our collective visions. Perhaps you will be moved to put on your shoes and set out—knowing that the planetary plan will work out only through our collective and coordinated footwork. We may gather our shared visions as we go. Let's set out to meet all our relations—as many as we can. Let's go about our walking work upon this Earth—not as a search for personal enlightenment or gain—but that we might feel our collective heartbeat.

SCENE ONE

The Farmer's
Mind Field

Seoul, Korea's capital city, was westernizing at an amazing rate during the years I was there. It seemed to change almost daily. Other cities were affected, but Seoul was the hub around which the country revolved. To really understand Korea, one of course had to know something of the ancient traditions which then still remained intact in the farms and the country villages. Yet the Korea of the moment—and of the future—could be seen in progress in the nation's capital. What I wanted most was to experience the Far East—to see and feel the philosophy and lifestyle of the ancient Orient. I did not like to think of ancient ways fading as the world was made uniform. But the process of westernization and modernization was inevitable, I knew, and I became involved in helping it happen. At least, I thought, it can happen in an atmosphere of mutual respect—and perhaps, eventually, as a mutual sharing between East and West.

I worked in Korea for nearly a decade. Early in my stay, I lived with a student I had met through a friend. We lived in a two-story house in a southeast suburb of Seoul, across the Han river from the city center where I worked. This student was from a farming village in the southern province of Chung Ang; but while he was attending a university in Seoul, he was living with his older sister and brother-in-law. The brother-in-law was attempting to buy this house, and as I was in need of a place to live, I decided to help out on the project by leasing the upstairs.

My college student friend was the youngest of many brothers and sisters, who all stayed home on the farm—except for himself and his oldest sister, who was married to an officer assigned to Seoul. According to Korean tradition, being the youngest in the family provided my friend an extra allotment of freedom. His was a huge extended family—a clan that was a village in itself—and all the population, other than the in-laws, had the same family name. I gave this friend a Western name, and he (with the help of his country father) gave me my Korean name. Here I will call him Jay.

Jay's father was the first son of the first son of the first son and so on—as far back as there were sons at all in that clan, and that fact gave him a practical and spiritual dominion over the whole vast family tree. He was king of the village. This particular patriarch was said to be an asset to his people. He was considered wise. He seldom ventured physically beyond the limits of a few dozen homes, fields, and rice paddies; but with a quiet, philosophical perspective, he pondered the nature and process of human affairs, and his people felt he understood the world. These villagers eagerly and often insistently placed every act and aspect of their lives before his judgment.

When Jay's mother reached her sixty-first year and thus began her second revolution of the astrological cycle (a very important birthday in Asian tradition), there was a big celebration down on the farm. Relatives came from all around and the entire village was involved. This occasion became my opportunity to meet Jay's country family. For such a special event, with so many traditional people, I would need to brush up on the customs I knew and learn the ones I did not.

So some training was in order. I had to learn, for one thing, how people meet people in farming villages of the

2

southern provinces of Korea. "You don't just stand there and bow," I was warned, "and you don't shake hands, because old Korean farmers have never seen that sort of thing. The old ones wouldn't know what to do with it. Or if they did know, they would consider it most impolite."

To execute the traditional low bow, it is necessary to kneel on the floor with the knees, hands, and head going down in the proper order—and in the precisely correct placement. I practiced this many times, hoping I would look sufficiently poised and natural when the time came to do it for real.

But when I arrived with my friend at his mud-brick, thatch-roofed house in the country, the old, bearded farmer was waiting—and he had been as well prepared for me as I had been for him. Bolt upright he stood, his golden eyes twinkling, and he thrust forward an open hand. But we did not shake hands. I at once lowered myself to my knees and bowed my head between my hands. And so he did the same. According to custom, there are polite phrases that ought to be spoken at times like this. I didn't say a word, although I had my greeting already prepared. I found it impossible to speak. The old man chuckled, trying to sound as gentle and kind as he could. That felt comforting and reassuring, and from that moment, in spite of having learned that there were those who nearly feared him, I sensed that we were friends.

"You have made a long journey with many hardships," he said. "It was so kind of you to come even though we have nothing good here at all."

I found it easy to speak with Jay's mother. She was a little woman who looked all of her sixty-one years. She showed me my sleeping place, which had been specially arranged with a mosquito net, and she, too, apologized in the typical traditional manner for my many hardships and for their poor home. As we talked, I noticed the bandage that bound her right hand. I remembered Jay's having told me about the time when the armies were fighting as far south as this farm and the villagers were scrambling up the hills in the dark of night. This frightened mother had lost her footing on a ridge and fallen down the slope. Her right hand had not functioned

3

since that day, but all the years since the war, with that crippled hand, she had been making clothes, cleaning floors, and thrashing rice.

Fortunately, there were countless friends and relatives here on this day, and she was waited on and not allowed to work. A little straw and bamboo hut had been set up in the hard clay-dirt patio behind this house especially for the festivities at hand, and in this hut the ladies of the village were cheerfully busy, working with vegetables, meats, nuts, leaves, roots, rice, bean curd, and a great abundance of garlic and peppers. Many friends and relatives had come from other towns and villages; and this family house, which was very large for a country home, was now crowded with people. I had been told I was the first Westerner ever to be a guest in this home or to visit this village.

Jay took me outside and led me through a grassy field until we were far away from all the noisy voices and confusion. "That's too many strange people for you," he said. "I think they are all looking at you too much."

The Korean countryside was charming. There in the meadow, there were no sounds at all but for a few birds chirping near a bubbly stream. We passed a few small, thatch-roofed houses that stood along the edge of the stream, walked upon the narrow paths that ran between the rice paddies, and then returned, just in time for supper.

A separate table had been set up in a little room for Jay and me and two of his brothers. There were dozens of these separate tables set up throughout the house and even in the hallways, and people ate in small groups.

After the meal, Jay's eldest brother suggested he take me outside again. Perhaps he did not feel I should be there for the cleaning-up process. Jay showed me the outdoor latrine, explaining that I should familiarize myself with the circumstances while there was sunlight to see by. This was the first time I had ever encountered an outhouse that was built over a pigsty. One could look down through the holes and see the snorting animals plodding to and fro below.

We strolled near the house until after sunset. The chirping of the crickets blended with the sound of countless voices

4

coming from inside. Through the windows we could see the flickering light of the oil lamps. We stood listening to the crickets until someone called out to say that everyone had gathered in the main sitting room. As we stepped in from the dark, the little candle-like flames of the many oil burners provided ample light—the rooms and hallways had a warm and comforting glow.

Jay and I appeared to be the last ones to enter the gathering room, which I had learned was called the friendship room in Korean. This room was as large as two average living rooms—and of course there was no furniture but a refreshment table and a multitude of cushions, and all these many people quite filled the room. This was to be a party, Jay had told me, a friendly social gathering to precede tomorrow's formal traditional ceremony.

Two children were standing at the father's shoulders, fanning him and holding at his reach a silver tray with grapes and rice wine. In this setting, he did indeed seem the village king. The old man slapped the floor and called for me to sit beside him. He held out his open palm with a chuckle and urged me to shake hands. Then he handed me a small cup and told one of the youngsters to fill it with rice wine. I turned my head away from him, and putting my chin over my shoulder, I lifted the cup to drink in the traditional Korean manner of drinking before elders.

He interrupted me with a tap on the shoulder and spoke one word in English: "Stop!" Then he leaned forward to look around me at his youngest son, who was sitting at my other side. He shouted in Korean. His tone was stern, but he was smiling. "What have you done to this poor fellow," he demanded, "giving all these instructions and restrictions on the first day? I don't want him to be afraid of me, I want him to come back!" He put his hand on my chin and turned my head to face his. "How can I say it in English—something like our 'ten thousand cheers?' "

"I don't know," Jay responded.

"Here's to your health," someone said.

"What? Speak up!"

"Here's to your health."

5

"No, no. That's too hard—I can't say that." He hit his cup against mine, making a loud clink and spilling a few drops of our wine; and then, grabbing hold of my wrist, he helped me dump the contents into my mouth. All the while I looked into his face. He seemed delighted. "Now tell our friend that I am going to speak about food, wine, and indulgence. Tell him that you will explain it later, and you must translate for him because he cannot understand."

He talked for a long time and in a lively manner, speaking in the siren-like intonation of the ancient Korean noblemen. He was right, I could not understand a word. When he had finished talking, he began to sing. It started softly with low, throaty tones so that at first I could not tell that it was going to be a song, but it became lively and lyrical and moved the old man to gesture and bob his head in the manner of a classical Korean dancer. He stopped, and there was total silence. All this while, no one had moved. He turned to me and said something like: "Well, I did all this to gain the right to insist that you offer us a song."

I was hesitant. I wondered what I could possibly offer that would qualify as a song in the view of this old traditional Korean. Jay's brother-in-law piped up, "Oh, Danny Boy!" He had heard me do it before.

"Good, good," the old man said the moment my song was over. "Now it becomes your right to appoint the next performer." He looked about the room, pondering the large number of visitors sitting on the floor. "But first I will take my leave so that you can all have a good time." He stood and walked slowly through the length of the room as people shuffled and scooted to make a path for him; stooping through a small sliding door at the back of the room, he disappeared. When he was out of sight, a few of the most elderly men stood and quietly exited through the same door.

This entire crowd was instantly transformed: there were very open—and very loud—sighs of relief, and the whole room burst into laughter. People uncrossed their legs, put their knees in the air, and fell back onto the people behind them. They lit cigarettes and poured wine and some even

6

began to toss grapes at one another. I was relieved of having to pick someone to sing.

"That's my father's inside room," Jay explained to me, "the one I told you about. Only a few times I have been called in there, but really it is his private meeting place for old men friends."

"Were people uncomfortable with him here?"

"Just it is difficult because our custom is too formal. We cannot play funny if he is here, and all the other people want to make a party. So he knows. Anyway, today he is much different. It is because of you, we think. We have never seen him take wine and sing a song before. It is first time for all these families and friends to see this. Even my mother has never seen it. Only he would do that in the inside room with old men friends. But it is so nice and interesting. It is why people made laughing when he went out."

"When he gave that talk—about wine and everything—I couldn't understand a word. What was that about? He said you'd explain it, right?"

"But I also could not understand. Sometimes he uses our ancient talking style. Really, I don't know what he said. Maybe just the old ones know. He was not talking about wine really. That was the outside talking for the inside topic." Jay called to his brother-in-law, who came to sit beside us. "My brother-in-law understands so much about deep philosophy. Maybe he can explain to me—then I will tell you in English."

The brother-in-law conversed with Jay for a while in what seemed like a thoughtful discussion of the old farmer's message, and then he crawled back across the floor to resume his place beside Jay's sister.

"No, we cannot explain it," Jay said.

"You mean you can't explain it in English?"

"No, it is not an explaining thing. We can't express it in any language. Brother-in-law says he can understand it, like a dream, but he cannot explain it. If he will try to explain it, then he also cannot understand."

"Is that what he told you?"

"Here, I will show you this way." With his fingertip, Jay made an imaginary diagram on the floor. He drew two circles and a line connecting them. "This one is our usual case, like our usual thinking place, and our mind will usually stay here. This other one is the place of deep understanding and our mind can sometimes go to there. But most people cannot go to that side—maybe only in sleep. Okay, but that deep understanding side does not contain anything like explanation or description. It is exactly deep reality with no description. So my brother-in-law said if he wants to explain, he must come to here, to explaining side—but then he cannot understand such like my father's talking. If he is on the understanding side, he can experience but he cannot make explanation, because if he tries to explain, it pulls him back out. This world is not real, he says, it is only a description of real. Understanding belongs to the real world, and explaining belongs to the unreal world. My brother-in-law, he cannot be in two worlds during same time—and so he cannot explain. Do you understand?"

"Yes, I think I do."

"In my father's case, this is always open." He moved his finger back and forth across the imaginary bridge between the two mental states or domains that we were visualizing. "We are knowing this about my father. He is here, and at the same time always here. Tonight's talking was a little strange because people want to make a party, and they cannot understand this kind of vocabulary. But my brother-in-law, he can understand. So he told me that my father's talking opens this bridge for the people so they can go to this side. My brother-in-law can follow. But he must be here or here—only one side at a time. He told me this, but I think you cannot understand."

"No, I think I do. I think I understand. But it's like you told me, the explanation is not important; it's the opening that counts. Still, I wish I could have understood the language. I couldn't even follow the outside part."

The birthday ceremony on the following day was indeed a formal affair—and it was highly ritualized—even some of the villagers, especially the young ones, had to be instructed in

8

the procedure as it went along. And it required most of the day, for every single individual present had to approach the mother on her throne-like seat, bow, and offer a cup of wine. She pretended to drink, but then she poured each cup into a basin behind her seat. I supposed this was the standard procedure: no one could make it through nearly one hundred cups of this homemade rice wine, especially at age sixty-one.

After the ceremony, people became playful again, poking, giggling, and chasing one another about the house. I had borrowed a camera for my trip to the country, and I wanted to get some pictures while there was some sunlight left. Every child and most of the villagers wanted to be in a picture. Then they wanted to be in a picture with me—not that they thought they would ever see it, but for my sake. So Jay used a few rolls of film taking these pictures. He took one of me in an old farmer's work hat and an A frame loaded with hay strapped to my back. I took some of him with his mother and another with his parents sitting together on the porch.

I requested a picture of the father sitting alone. He went inside and then reappeared a few moments later wearing a beautiful traditional Korean suit made of silk brocade with gold threads. It had a white silk jacket and a vest with gems for buttons. The mother brought out his tall black horsehair hat, his long-stemmed pipe, and an elegantly painted hand fan. The old patriarch sat on his cushion and posed. After sunset, he sat in his own special room and called for Jay to come in for a private conversation.

The following day, Jay talked to me about that conversation as we rode on the northbound train on our way back to Seoul. It was very rare for him to be invited into his father's private space—many of his family had never been in that room—and Jay supposed it happened partly because he was in college and living away and partly because he had come with me. Now that his father had met me, Jay felt, he was prepared to appreciate his living in Seoul and to be more understanding of his changing ways. So they had had a very amiable chat about his college and his plans.

"Anyway, he is so kind and gentle to me, compared to others," Jay said, "because I am the youngest son, and this is our custom in our country families. He loves me so much, even he never says it directly. He does so many things to prove it, and so he wants me to feel it. You know, he always surprises me—and this time, he surprised everyone. We never saw him like this before."

"You mean like singing in front of the whole crowd of guests?"

"And he never had his picture before. You are the first one to have his picture. You are the only one. Even at the family weddings he avoided it. He never allowed his picture to be taken by anyone."

"I really didn't know that," I said. "Maybe I should not have asked—or you should have told me."

"No, he was okay for it."

"Why do you think he was so willing?"

Jay had asked him about that during their private meeting, and now he described to me what his father had told him. Jay had been too curious and too puzzled not to bring it up. So he had asked his father if he had shaken my hand and offered the wine and the lecture and the song to make a favorable impression on an American. And he had questioned him as to why he had allowed me two pictures even when he had refused his own family on special occasions.

"I don't make any laws," his father had answered. "I never did. I don't have my own rules—not for me or you or anyone. I just follow the laws of my country, the laws of nature, and the ways of our ancient traditions. In every case I just simply fit in. I am not needed in the family pictures. It adds nothing, but it rather subtracts from the others. I do as I do only to fit what I am. I am a first son who is the principal heir to this large farm by our ancient custom, and I must do as I am expected. If I have any preferences of my own which do not fit, I must be willing to change them. So I control my preferences. If I should one day have to live in America, you would be surprised how nicely I could change.

"I never preferred to have my picture taken. All my family has always known this, so there has never been a problem with this preference. This afternoon I did something that I

10

had not done in the past—and I did it willingly. When you are a man, you may do as you wish. But for myself, I will avoid only one thing—and it is not the camera. I will avoid fixed preferences. It is foolish to have preferences which stubbornly stick where they clearly do not fit and overtake even one's own good will and judgment!"

Some time after our return from our visit to Jay's family home, he had occasion to make the trip again. This time, he went alone, and in quite a rush and fury, making the ten-hour trip south by train with a sudden need to speak to his father about an urgent family matter.

One young woman who lived in that village—Jay's second cousin—was begging permission to marry a modern dilet-tante who lived in Seoul. The would-be lovers had met only briefly at some village event, and this cavalier man had pro-posed. It was not the traditional way. Besides, he was too old and sophisticated for this young country cousin. The villagers sought the judgment of my friend's venerable old father—but the old patriarch said nothing.

I learned about the whole situation one day when Jay received a letter from the village. By now I had been living for some months in this house in Seoul with Jay and his sister and brother-in-law, and I was having most of my meals with them. They had become like a family.

"My cousin is coming up here on the train from the country to spend a couple days here with us," Jay told me. "Her real reason is to see this bad man who lives here in Seoul—I know that. But my sister says we have to welcome her here, and we even have to invite this man for dinner so they can meet again. Imagine, we have to let them meet in our house. I do not understand why they allow this. My father could stop it. If he would only speak his mind, he could stop the whole thing."

At his sister's insistence, Jay agreed to go into the city early on the day his cousin was to arrive. He was told to reach this man before he left for work. "I am the one who has to

11

tell him that his 'girlfriend' is coming," Jay complained. "But really, I don't even want to see him. It becomes my duty. I have to obey my sister. So, I will give him his dinner invitation. After that, I'll go directly to the station and wait for my cousin to arrive on the train. If the train's not late, maybe we'll be here by lunchtime."

He returned home stunned and without his cousin. He had found her already at that man's house. When he had knocked on the door, they had appeared in their night clothes. She had come on a previous train, and they had spent the night together.

Jay prepared at once to set out for his village. His innocent experience did not permit even the thought of such an affair, and he was compelled to report it to his father. "My father will be angry now," he assured me. "This is not right in my country. Now he will stop this thing at once and they will never see each other again."

But things turned out otherwise. Jay returned surprisingly quickly and announced that he had spent barely an hour in his hometown, not more than half that time with his father, had spoken but a few words, and had not explained a thing. The marriage would happen. It would not be called off.

Jay told the whole story. By the time he had reached his village train station, he had built up such an anger that he raced across the meadow and ran stumbling into the house. No one was inside. Again he raced, looking for his father, through the fields and along the paths that ran between the rice paddies. He found the old farmer in one of these paddies, shin-deep in water, tending to his young plants.

"Father, Father! I have to talk to you!"

"Ho! What? You want to talk when you can hardly breathe?" He sat down on the bank, lit a match, and calmly touched it to a leech that was attached to his ankle. "Do not talk now. You would be a nuisance to listen to. They say a swallow of something helps in a case like this, and I am thirsty myself. Go to the house and bring us back a teakettle of cool barley tea."

When Jay returned with the tea, he was still running and still out of breath. "Father, I have to tell you something."

"You will say nothing. You will sit down here and calm yourself. Now pour the tea here on the ground."

"Pardon me, Father?"

"Has your hearing left you as well as your composure?"

"No, but I don't understand. I thought you said to—"

"I told you to say nothing, that's what. And I told you to pour the tea onto the ground. If you do not trust either your senses or mine, you had better return at once."

Jay let spill a few drops onto the ground.

"All of it! All of it! Pour it!"

He emptied the contents of the teakettle and watched the cool barley tea sink into the soil.

"Now! Shall we have our drink?"

"But Father, I just—"

"What is the matter with you? Why do you not fill my cup?"

"Father, how can I?"

"Because I am asking you. Because I am expecting my tea!"

"Father, how do you expect me to get the tea back out of the ground?"

"Aha! Then perhaps you can learn something here. What do you expect me to do about that situation that has happened up in Seoul? How can I reverse it?"

My friend sat quietly beside his father and stared at the ground. "Father, may I ask you something?"

"You may."

"Forgive me, sir, but it appears to my mind you could have stopped those two before it came to this."

"Stop it? Why should I stop it? That relationship is like a chestnut falling from a tree. The moment you and I come to witness such a thing, the chestnut has long prepared to let go of the branch. There is no way to keep it there. There is no way to return it. Every occurrence is but a link in a chain —a sequence of causes and effects. That you are my son and I am your father—this situation was a long time arranging. Two people may believe they are meeting for the first time, while a deeper perception will tell us they have met long before. Their involvement, for better or for worse, may be long in its history."

13

"But this is fate, Father, and you have always said—"

"Fate? Look at these young plants! When this rice is in our bowls, shall we call it fate? Clearly we can see the coming of choice, the process of action, and the moment of result. But human affairs become complex, and chains of events, when people do not guide them, seem to spin in circles. People become confused as to what is the planting and what is the harvest. Everything is a matter of choice. Everything. And then there are results, and further choices at every turn. The question is with whom lies which choice, and what is to be chosen. Sometimes we fail to recognize the moment of choice. Sometimes we fail to understand the process of playing out."

The old farmer stood up and waded into the rice paddy. "The northbound train is passing soon. Go and concentrate on your studies."

◐   ◐   ◐

Of the few photographs I took during all my years in Korea, I would have valued most the one I shot of Jay's parents and the one of his father sitting on the porch in his finest traditional silk suit. But I eventually decided there was no point in keeping them. When I had first had them developed in Seoul and examined them through my battery-lighted viewer, I was disappointed to find that the old farmer's face was blurred. Jay and I could recognize him well enough, but the out-of-focus effect rather spoiled the pictures. Those who knew photography better than I puzzled at these pictures: it was virtually impossible for only the farmer's face to be out of focus in such otherwise clear pictures. What was at first a disappointment became a mystery. The man's face continued to change over time—right on my slides—until there was no longer any face at all. It was as though I had captured a headless man in a horsehair hat. Between the white jacket and the black hat, there was only space. I showed these slides to several people, explaining that after I took the pictures, I discovered that the old man had never before allowed himself to be photographed. Everyone agreed that, whether by his very nature, by some uncon-

14

scious intentionality on his part, or by pure coincidence, the old man's lifelong priority had prevailed after all—while all my other shots had turned out fine. Over time, his image disappeared entirely, clothes and all, and only the mother remained. But eventually, after several years, she too was gone, and I had only smoky clouds mounted in 35 millimeter frames.

Those pictures are gone but I still have my memory—and my memory serves me better, in any case, than the slides could have done. That venerable old farmer was not the sort of person one forgets. My mind holds the image, and it never fades. Anytime I wish, there he sits in his traditional clothing, with his long-stemmed pipe and his tall black horsehair hat, and I can clearly picture his wispy white beard, high cheekbones, and tigerlike eyes. In fact, I can recall the old farmer in a larger context than had been captured in my photos. In my mental pictures I see not only the old man's image but also his milieu. His appearance, his manner, his lifestyle, and his cultural setting—as well as all the implications and responsibilities implied by his cultural tradition—all these remain clear in my memory.

◐　　　◐　　　◐

A photograph, of course, has a very limited contexture. It has a frame—or, at least, edges. That may be why no one else had a photograph of the old farmer. There was much about him that could not be taken out of context. He had talked in that crowded room that night—sharing his philosophy while everyone else had listened so attentively—and no one had been able to capture and hang onto a concrete explanation of what he had said. But an explanation is a categorizing, a pigeonholing. There is no context or sequence to an explanation.

There is a great deal in this world that cannot be understood through analysis—through a separating out. Reality cannot be cut and cropped and contained within borders. An out-of-context picture fades. The old farmer had a sense of sequence that was as sure and steady as the unfolding seasons.

Few people these days are in a cultural position like that of the old farmer. Not many, in fact, live in a physical environment like his. One's earthly circumstance does not automatically make one a mystic or a visionary. But it can help. The mystic can become apparent in anyone who attains a sufficient degree of perception and composure. The old farmer had a vast contexture. He could shake hands with a different culture, if he wished, and fit in as he saw fit. But he could not be captured or contained.

In my recollections of the villages and farmlands, it seems easy to see scenarios and not just set scenes—and easy to sense a scheme in the scenarios. The morning roosters, the evening crickets, the steady, stretching fields and meadows, and the seasonal winds and rains—these present an often predictable but always progressing picture. It is a picture with an abundance of contexture, and it is easy to follow the flow.

But you don't have to be down on the farm to see seasons and cycles or to develop a sense of sequence and synchronicity. Cause and effect are everywhere. All that is is connected and related; the constant interplay of life goes on in every corner of the universe.

The mystic's perspective is of an unframed and ever-growing context—an ongoing continuum—in terms of both time and space. Within this context—and it is not fate but a constant, creative flow—every living being is a consciously functioning factor. From the mystic's perspective, you can see yourself as a player in an infinitely unfolding drama. From the mystic's perspective, you realize you are essential to the whole production because if you were to drop out or drop dead, it would change the whole scenario. (Dropping out is impossible, of course, in the big picture. You are always playing some role somewhere in the picture.) You realize that you are actually a coauthor of the entire production. As coauthor, you are free to play yourself however you see fit; but it is always to your advantage (and everyone else's) if what you do makes sense within the context of the whole scenario. It is a mutual creation. The cast may expect you to come up with ideas for the script. Options and opportunities appear in every scene—and to every player—but always within the context of the whole ongoing collaboration. Of course, every drama unfolds forwards: there is no going back and undoing what has already been played out.

You therefore consider the cast and the script and the ongoing scenario. You consider consequences of the past and choices of the present—and which choices belong to whom. You must thus perceive the roles of the other players—and learn to focus not only upon your own monadic moment but also upon the broad, unframed perspective. Then you must still play your own part—and play it from the present moment forward.

So the old farmer sits back and folds his arms and watches the tea sink into the ground. The mystic's perspective is available to everyone, and the old farmer endeavors to invoke it in his youngest son. They sit at the edge of the rice paddy—under the chestnut tree—to contemplate what one can do with the present moment. They cannot put the tea back in the pot—nor the chestnuts on the ground back on the tree. They cannot undo what has already transpired with the couple up in Seoul. Thus the old farmer tells his son to put his heart into his own present moment and play his own perspective.

◑   ◑   ◑

But what really happened to my slides? What caused them to disappear? What could have been responsible that they should fall out of focus and eventually fade away? One wonders—and there are several ways to deal with wondering: forget it, deny it, indulge in it, or figure it out.

The old farmer did not likely conjure up some coy trick to ruin my slides. If he had the wizardry, he had not the need, for he need not have troubled to pose in the first place. The farmer didn't do anything to my photos. They did it to themselves. The farmer posed and let it go at that, but he was who he was, and my slides reacted. All those years of constant, focused intent had produced a potent image—too powerful for my exposures to endure—and they eventually departed.

17

This gives some sense of how much impact one single individual's life and will can have upon the field of mind. There can be no escaping the fact that all things, however great or small, exert some measure of effect (however great or small) upon all other things. We are walking about in a mind field—composed of an infinite accumulation of images, impressions, and intentions—wherein all the little particles of life impact and influence one another. All that is manifest meets and mixes within the mind field, moving constantly toward greater mutuality. All along the way, different individuals insert varying degrees of influence into the mind field—and the more potent the individual's input, the more potent the impact upon the mind field.

Often single individuals such as Mohandas K. Gandhi or Martin Luther King, Jr. can quite knowingly make an impact upon the mind field that ripples and reverberates across the world and throughout history. Both Mahatma Gandhi and Dr. King were attentive to a collective consciousness, and it was from this perspective that they promoted the principle of right relations. But whether consciously or unconsciously, whether helpfully or harmfully, all living beings exert some measure of impact upon the collective mind.

The old farmer was a very savvy and practical mystic. He knew, as all mystics have always known, that all things are alive and all life is related. He knew himself to extend beyond his boundaries, and yet it was his way to fit in. The righteous execution of the duties of his position called for this, and his experience and his very nature (and perhaps these are the same) provided it. He did not affect what did not reside within his sphere of relativity: it was his own personal image that faded from my photos (that of his wife followed), while all my other photographs turned out and lasted.

The old farmer spent his lifetime farming in the mind field. He did it with integrity. He worked with nature and the seasons. It was his responsibility and his contribution. And it was to the benefit of his relations. He understood well the planting, the growing, and the harvest.

18

SCENE TWO

No Shame—No Blame

Koh was a young college graduate who often came around our office to visit with a former schoolmate who was part of our Korean staff. Koh loved to talk, and he often sat beside my desk, engaging me in conversation when I ought to have been doing something else. My colleagues and I managed an institute in Seoul for training Korean government and corporation employees in business and language skills. Koh was working as a botanist in a nursery on the other side of the city, but he seemed to have ample free time to make frequent trips across town to spend hours visiting in our office. Often we sat in one of the tearooms in our building or across the street. In Korea, people had their conversations in tearooms, whether for business or for pleasure. Koh claimed to have many "Western" acquaintances, and his English was almost adequate and very abundant.

I was impressed with his outgoing manner: he greeted absolutely everyone and with the slightest excuse, struck up a conversation, whether in English or Korean, as though everyone were already his friend. Yet, in his own language, which offered various options of usage from the very formal to the very familiar, he nearly always employed the most polite sentence structure, even in circumstances in which most others did not.

I ran into Koh one time on a busy downtown street when he was shoving a young boy through the crowds, holding the boy's arm twisted behind his back. In his free hand the boy held a wallet, and I knew right away what had happened. Koh had caught a young pickpocket. He was so intent upon his business that he did not notice me, but I reversed my direction and followed along behind. I could hear him talking to the boy. His tone was reassuring and anything but blameful, and I could tell he was speaking in a manner appropriate for addressing a peer and not a youngster—especially not one of these street kids that everyone called slicky boys. The man whose wallet had been picked was waiting on the corner. Apparently he had seen that the boy was caught. The man did not look angry but only pleased to repossess his property—an extremely rare occurrence—and the boy bowed again and again and repeated his apologies.

Koh was embarrassed when he saw me. "I wasn't going to hurt him."

"I knew you weren't hurting him," I said. "I know you'd never hurt anyone."

"If I have to hurt him, I just let him go," Koh continued, "even if he gets away. I never hurt anyone again."

"I'm sure you've never hurt a soul in your life," I said. "I don't think you could." He seemed physically capable of doing so. He was a small person, but he looked like a compact version of a weightlifter or an athlete.

"Never again. It is my promise."

"Why, have you ever hurt anyone before?" I asked, realizing at once that it was a thoughtless question.

"Anyway, no more." Koh looked uncomfortable, as though in his excitement he had said something he regretted.

"What did you say to that kid?" I asked, changing the subject.

"I told him he should never be ashamed himself."

"Should never be? You said that? Most people would say he ought to be ashamed of himself for stealing."

20

"No, he is already ashamed, so I told him that. He wanted that he doesn't go back to the man. I said to him if it's money, I help with money. But it was because he is too much ashamed. So I told him if he gives back the wallet then the shame can reduce. He has to respect himself more—not be so much ashamed himself every day. If he has respect for himself, such a boy cannot steal. You know how these boys think themselves? The most low people. They are too ashamed themselves already. That's the problem."

One evening I went with him to visit his aunt, who lived on a hilltop at the edge of the city. Though I could not recall exactly what in our conversations might have accounted for it, Koh was taking me to see this aunt because she was a *mudang*—a Korean shaman—and he had decided I would be interested.

I had never met or spoken with a mudang but I had heard a bit about them. In fact, I had actually heard them, more than once, noisily at work throughout the night in Korean households in the neighborhood where I lived. Their constant drumming was loud and harsh. It sounded to me as though people were pounding on pots and pans with metal spoons—with maybe a few bells and cymbals in the background. Yet the noise was rhythmic and exciting and somehow so exhilarating that I did not mind being forced to lie awake listening for hours. The Korean people with whom I lived avoided explaining. Perhaps they knew little about the mudang and their rituals, or perhaps they thought an American would think them too bizarre. Since the local people were quite adept at keeping track, over a considerable area, of the affairs of their neighbors, I usually learned when someone had passed away, suffered a loss, or sought to bestow blessing upon a coming birth or a business venture. I discovered that there were many more willing to call upon the mudang's services than to openly discuss their belief in them.

We got off the bus just outside the great ancient gate that once, long ago, was a guarded doorway in a great wall,

21

marking the western boundary of the city of Seoul. The sun began to set behind us as we started along the path that led up the hill. I felt a need to question my friend about these mudang—since I was about to meet one.

"Well, people don't know they should believe it or not," Koh explained as we walked along, turning back occasionally to see the deep red glow of the sunset. "It requires that we believe in spirits and souls around us, and it is supposed to be denied in modern times. Now we try to westernize everything. People like to say they only keep it as a custom—just we enjoy our ancient ways—but really they feel big expectation on these mudang when they get some problems and emergencies."

"But what about the mudang themselves?" I asked. "The people who are getting paid to serve these expectations— what do they believe? Do they think they're just satisfying some old customs?"

"Pay? They don't receive much like you might think. Most of them are poor. The people prepare much food for making offering like for ancestors or something, and after the mudang finished their doings, they could get the food."

"But what do these mudang do? And what do they themselves believe? Do they believe in the spirits and souls?"

"So anyway, my aunt is mudang, right? I'm not mudang so we have to ask it to her. I will ask it whatever you like and I will tell you in English after she's explain."

We heard a strange, steady thumping sound ahead of us. It was nearly dark now and I could not see into the distance. For a very brief moment, there flashed through my mind some vague images of spirits or souls trying to make their presence known to us. This was owing, I supposed, to our conversation.

But Koh knew immediately what this was, or so he claimed. "I will show you," he said, smiling, as though he thought I was about to see something interesting. He turned his head about in the darkness to locate the sound and pointed downhill, off to our right. "Come on! I will show you!"

I would not have caught sight of the young soldier even in daylight, for he was behind us and the sounds I had heard

22

were echoes thumping off the wall of a building in front of us. We stepped off the path and felt our way downhill, and when we were only a few yards away, we sat down on the slope to watch. The soldier's skin nearly blended into the darkness, but I could quite clearly see the sleeves of his uniform and thus follow his movements. He was hitting his hands against a board, about the size of a two-by-four, that was somehow solidly secured or perhaps buried in the ground.

"Is he doing that with his bare hands?" I questioned. Each hit produced a loud, sharp crack. It seemed impossible.

"Shh!" Koh whispered, nodding his head. Apparently, he did not want the man to know we were watching.

As my eyes adjusted to the near-darkness, I could see the man's hands. He held them flat and stiff and he rotated his wrists as he thrust his arms, one after the other, so that his palms turned up just as he connected. He was striking the board at hip level, and with the tips of his fingers, it seemed. It was a somewhat disturbing sight. Somehow he was hitting with unbelievable force, and I felt an empathetic pain in my hands and chest with each loud crack.

He paused and shook his hands at his sides. Then he looked up and saw us. He stood stark still and stared at us. I felt certain, after what I had seen, that he could not have been alarmed. Perhaps he was offended. I wanted Koh to say something, but we both remained silent. Then the man smiled, and it felt reassuring. Now his large white teeth shining in the darkness were the most visible part of him.

Why didn't Koh say something? "Good evening," I called out, to my own surprise.

I heard him gasp softly. "English man," he mumbled, and he stooped to pick up his army cap and walked away.

"Koh, why didn't you talk to him?" I regretted having used English, but I thought since we had been watching, we ought to have spoken. "You usually speak to everyone."

"Sometimes we should not talk," Koh answered, still whispering. "In such a case we don't say something."

"Why not?"

"He is enough strong he cannot disturb by our looking. If

he watches us a few minutes, we don't move and we don't talk. He can forget us. Then he continues. The feeling is we are nothing here because we don't change anything. To talk is a kind of catch somebody. They become taken into our doing. Because they have to talk some answer, then we have to talk again. In his practice he have to keep it—his doing mind—what do you call? You say his own mind intention? This can be disturbed by our talking because we are outside of his practice. I cannot explain completely."

"No, I understand. But he did smile at us."

"Maybe he thinks you looked funny."

"No," I said, "it was a friendly smile."

"Anyway, he cannot speak English, I think, and he is afraid of Westerner."

"Afraid? You called him strong."

"You see, in your country you have every kind of people: Asian, European, Indian, black, red, yellow, everything. In here, we have only one kind. For some Koreans it is a big thing to make a contact to a foreigner. Anyway, for you it would be good to know such a kind of people. This training is very interesting for you, I think." He stood up and walked over to where the soldier had been. "Look at this," he said, examining the board.

I looked. The board had been worn nearly halfway through at the place where the man had been hitting. "Did he do this? Did he do all this with his fingers?"

"Not just tonight only, I don't think so. They do it for a long time. Maybe other people used it, too." He made a pose as though he were about to strike the board himself. "Now I can break it, though. I will show you. I can take off the top in only one time hitting." He made a lunge and stopped himself abruptly, nearly losing his balance. "Do you see over there? It's a kind of barracks. They are something like MP, I think. Anyway, this belongs to them, I should not destroy it." But he held his hand to the board, apparently still tempted to try it. "Maybe it's okay, I show you one time. They can change it anyway and put new board."

He stood motionless for a moment. I thought he might be making himself ready. But he turned abruptly and started up the hillside. "Let's go!" he said. "They might come out."

I felt relieved. I was sure he could not have broken the board, but he could have hurt himself trying.

"I wanted to show you," he said, as we reached the path again. "I think it's interesting to you."

"Do you really think you could have done that?" I asked.

"I don't know. I quit."

We walked slowly now along the uphill path. It was dark and quiet. The little houses along the ridge above us glowed like Oriental lanterns as candlelight shone through their translucent rice-paper doors and windows.

"Last year I stopped it," Koh went on. "Before that I practiced so many years. Do you see? Look at this!"

He held out his hands and I peered at them in the darkness.

"No, no. You check my fingers!"

They felt almost unreal. If these hands had not been warm, I could have imagined they were artificial—made of plastic or hard rubber. "Then why didn't you try breaking the board?"

"I told you I don't do it anymore. It's not for me. I don't explain the reason."

I did not pursue the matter. In any case, the way was steeper now and narrow, and we had to walk single file and with some concentration. The path had been terraced in places, but often the ground slipped beneath my feet.

Suddenly, Koh turned and put out a hand to hold me back. It felt like a warning. I tried to see whether something was in the path ahead.

"Did you take pig meat?"

"What? What do you mean?"

"I forgot to mention about something. If you took any meat of pig whole day, we cannot get in there."

I could have simply told him that I had not eaten any meat at all, but his questioning both startled and intrigued me. "Why not?" I asked, causing him to doubt not only whether he could justify his aunt's unusual ways, but also whether, for her sake, he ought to take a chance on me. It seemed

25

that I, as a stranger, and a foreigner at that, could easily create a disturbance in this house—particularly to this mudang's spirit helpers. It would be especially bad if I had recently consumed any pork or liquor. I assured him I'd had neither meat nor liquor; but now, for the first time, I began to wonder how she would feel about an American visitor. Koh had no way to reach her, and she could not know I would be coming.

"Maybe I check first," Koh said. "Okay, you wait here. I never took somebody over here before. Just I'll go check it up and I'll come back."

But I feared he might be gone for a long time, and I did not want to be left alone in the dark standing on this path.

"It takes a few minutes," he said. "It's just over there."

"Quickly, quickly!" someone shouted in Korean from the distance. "Come quick, you rascal, and bring your foreign friend!"

"My God, it's my aunt!"

The woman appeared, shuffling down the path, carrying a flashlight. "What kind of friend are you, anyway?" She shined her light in his face.

"Have you been in peace?" Koh said, in the customary greeting.

But she went on scolding him, hitting him on the back in a playful manner. I could understand only part of what she said, but in spite of her words, her tone was warm and friendly. Briefly, she put the beam on me and then quickly moved it, as though she had suddenly thought better of it. I had not minded. I knew she wanted to see my face—and I also wanted to see hers, I realized. As though she'd read my thoughts, she held the light upon herself and smiled at me. Until that moment, I had been unaware of my preconceived image of this woman. She had the round, full-cheeked appearance that is sometimes called moonface, and I realized I had unconsciously been imagining a sharp face with a beaked nose and a pointed chin. Her head was covered with a scarf whose pointed corner came down over her forehead between her eyebrows; in the beam of her flashlight, her wide smile seemed to take up half her face. Her strange gesture was friendly. Yet, I felt awkward standing there watching her, thinking I should speak but not knowing what to say. Again she scolded her nephew, aiming her light in his eyes and making him squint. Then she turned and guided herself along the path, leaving us to follow.

"She keeps saying I made you feel bad. She told me if she can speak English she will invite you inside without me because our way is not accustomed for you and I only make you feel some difficulties. She's joking me a little, but anyway, I am sorry. It's my responsibility to make you feel easy. She says you do not worry yourself about anything."

"It's all right," I responded. "I'm okay. Don't you worry, either."

The mudang's house was only a few minutes further along the path. Surrounded by a high fence with a large wooden gate, it was invisible from the outside. The house looked rather small and humble for such a high fence and impressive gate. It was a traditional-style house: a split-level arrangement with sliding doors and windows, two rooms just above ground level and a sunken, dirt-floor kitchen whose perpetual cooking fires heated the flues that passed under the covered flagstone floor of the main room. A small hand pump in the center of the courtyard provided the water, and for light there were tall, flickering oil lamps that sat on the floor. Inside there was no furniture except the typical standing closet that held the sleeping mats and bedding, a small black lacquer table that hung on the wall near the steps that led down into the kitchen, and a plywood board placed atop some standing crates for a makeshift shelf. On this shelf sat a stuffed bird that looked like a raven; it cast on the wall a dark shadow that wiggled from the flickering flames of the oil lamps. Under the shelf were large glass jars filled with dried leaves and berries and ginseng roots. There were many big puffy cushions on the floor, and on one of them lay a fat grey cat who also appeared stuffed until it twitched an ear in its sleep. The heavy, honey-colored oil paper that covered the flagstone floor had been roasted brown in spots

27

through many winters of heat from the kitchen's coal fires. Now, when early autumn evenings were only slightly cool, the cookstove dampers were turned so that the emissions from the perpetually burning coal bricks would be vented outside and not heat the floor. In such kitchens there is always a large kettle of water keeping hot on the coals, and as soon as we were comfortable on our cushions, the lacquer table was taken from its hook on the wall, and tea was prepared.

"So!" said Koh abruptly, the moment our tea was poured. "Go ahead. Ask your questions for my aunt. You told me you have some questions about mudang."

I pondered. It would appear too forward, I thought, to sit here and ask questions, as though I had come to find out something.

But the aunt spoke up. "Leave him alone!" she reprimanded. Either she had understood Koh's English or she had sensed my feeling. Then she went on with that same sort of scolding that Koh had to translate.

"She told me I have the same mistake every time because I make you feel strange in this situation."

She spoke again.

"On the other hand," Koh translated, "if you have anything to talk, it's okay. She is okay for anything so you don't worry yourself. Anyway, she might go out suddenly because there's one old grandmother over there on that hill, she might be dying now. Maybe soon they call to my aunt."

But she continued and she went on talking for a long time, gesturing and questioning and pausing at times for her nephew's acknowledgment. She had a single cigarette in a tiny metal box which she lit and put out repeatedly as we sat.

"She is a kind of my teacher," Koh explained. "She is always making this understanding to me. Now she told about that boy. By herself she knows about it. Do you remember? You saw it when I caught that slicky—" He stopped himself. "And we shouldn't say slicky boy, even everybody else do. That's the problem to such a people. Everybody gives more shame to them. I told you, right? Really he is already ashamed. I catch him for himself. It was not more for the man than for the boy, because he has to improve his feeling to himself. This kind of philosophy belongs to my aunt. So she said in connection that I have responsibility to make you comfortable in here, and never hard time. She thinks in that way. Do you understand?"

"Sure," I said. "Is this philosophy part of the mudang tradition?"

"I don't know so many mudang. Just now I ask to her, okay?" He did, and she responded, and through the discussion that ensued, she wove for me her answer.

First she spoke to Koh and then she questioned me, pointing at him. I understood somewhat but was not sure how to answer, so she gestured for him to explain.

"She asked you if do you know why I showed you my fingers. Remember? She knows it. Just tonight I showed you. She asked you can you get any meaning from it?"

"Like what?"

"No, why do you hesitate? Maybe you can know I practiced for a long time. Tang su do, tae kwon do, everything. I didn't tell you, but you know. Actually, I told you I stopped. I quit it. She thinks you might wonder this thing about me."

"I might have wondered a little. I really didn't think much about it."

"Anyway, she is pushing me to tell you about it. I never say about this thing to anybody. Only to her, because she helps me. She says you can understand me about this, so I have to tell it to you."

He appeared to wait for my encouragement. "Please tell me, I'd like to hear about it," I said, though I had no idea what it was. So I was told the whole surprising story in full detail.

Several months earlier, Koh and a friend of his had rented a couple of trail bikes and ridden out to spend a weekend in a remote area a few miles north of the city. On their first night there, after they had set up their tent and finished their campfire supper, they tried their skill on the trail bikes, maneuvering the bumpy trail that went along the side of the mountain. They came to a dirt road and decided to take it back down the hill so they could enjoy some smoother riding and a little speed; but as they turned onto the road, they noticed a car parked off to the side a few yards ahead. They could see by the moonlight that there were people inside, and the people appeared to be fighting. They rode on a ways, thinking they should not interfere or become involved; but then Koh stopped and urged his friend to go back with him. He was quite certain that one of those people was a teenage girl. She might be needing help.

They turned around and rode back up the hill, pulling up beside the driver's window. There were two men and one girl inside the car. The man behind the wheel had his hand over the girl's mouth. Her clothes were torn. The driver rolled down his window and gave Koh's friend a shove, shouting at them to mind their own business, and the other man kept repeating, "Let's go, let's go!" Impulsively, Koh jumped for the car and yanked open the driver's door. The man climbed out, releasing the girl, and she began to scream, "Help me! Help me!" The man was huge and he was drunk and looked crazed. He made a lunge for Koh. Koh ducked, and the man grabbed hold of his hair, pulling hard. Koh made a defensive stab, striking the man in the ribs, and he could feel his hand inside the man's body, nearly to the wrist. For a moment, they both stood dazed. Then Koh pulled his hand free, and the man dropped to the ground.

There was total panic. There they were, miles from anywhere. The man was moaning and bleeding on the ground. The girl jumped out and started to run, but she tripped on her tattered clothes and fell on her face, sobbing hysterically. Koh's friend carried her back to the car and insisted that they all get in and rush for help. But they could not move the injured man and they could not leave him.

Koh struggled to regain his presence of mind. He ran around and pulled the other man out of the car, suddenly realizing that if the man could drive, he might decide to make a getaway and leave them stranded. But this was a smaller and younger man, and he looked frightened and helpless. Even if he could drive this car, he was now totally dazed and incoherent. And Koh had made matters worse by pulling him out of the car to where he could see his injured companion, who now lay in a puddle of blood and appeared to be either unconscious or dead. The moaning had stopped, and Koh could not tell whether he was breathing.

The girl lay in the back seat sobbing. There was no one who could drive the car down the hill to phone for help. Koh's friend decided to try it, though he had almost no knowledge of driving. They would leave Koh and the girl there with the injured man. Then there occurred what Koh thought must have been a miracle. They were struggling to get the girl out of the car and the other man in, when a rickety truck came rattling down the road.

They stood in its path and forced it to stop. The little man inside was old and nearly deaf; and it took him a long time to comprehend the situation, for at first he had thought he was being robbed. "I have no money," he kept pleading, "only sacks of beans from my poor little farm."

Finally, Koh's friend and the other man were on their way down the hill, sitting in the back of the truck with the sacks of dried beans, and Koh and the girl were left with the injured man, waiting for an ambulance. When the sound of the truck had faded, and there was silence, Koh could hear, to his great relief, that the man was breathing.

"Do you want him to live or to die?" Koh asked the girl. "If you don't want him to die, you have to help me pray for him. It's the only thing we can do." So they prayed aloud. The girl calmed down and began to think of helping. She suggested they should use a piece of her torn dress to hold over the open wound and her jacket to help keep him warm. They prayed together until the ambulance arrived.

"Three days I sat in hospital," Koh said, "and even that girl, too." He stopped. His story was finished. All during his telling he had been staring at the floor, and now he looked up as if to observe my reaction. "So that's the reason," he concluded.

"The reason you quit training?"

"That's why I quit it everything. I made promise myself I never hit anybody. Never again—not for practice, not even for defend myself."

For a moment I considered the significance of what he had

told me. But the story was not complete. "What happened to that man?" I asked.

"Now he is okay," Koh said. "No, not okay, but getting almost okay now. It's healing for a long time." He held his hand in front of his face. "With this I broke his ribs and everything. And he had bleeding inside. Inside and outside bleeding. So during a long time I went to hospital almost every day, and the girl, too. That other man, he was her neighbor, so they had acquaintance just a little. That's why she went inside the car. But they were so drunk and crazy. So this aunt she helped us for everything. Not for hospital things—for our spirit. She said this problem is because losing contact of our spirit. We get away from inside spirit. We have a kind of shame, so we have to break up the shame, or it just can go around. I think that's why she pushed me to let you know the story. I told you, it's her philosophy."

"But did she actually do something? I mean about the shame?"

"Sometimes she did explaining for us, and sometimes contact to the spirit—even sing a song for that. Is it strange for you? Some parts I cannot explain. At first, the man doesn't like it, but he wants to heal up everything. So we join together. My aunt says he is too fat and walking funny, and he is always drunken. He become to hate himself. So it begins the problem and it goes to the girl and the other man. If this thing happens to any girl and woman—even she couldn't help it and could not avoid for that—she will become ashamed to herself. That's what my aunt said so. So this thing can grow to worse and worse because from the beginning this man already think himself no good. Hate oneself. That's the first problem of the society, she said, for sick and crime or everything. That's why I told you. If someone respect himself, he cannot do such kind of these things.

"So anyway, it also went to me because I hurt him so serious. Nobody can know how much I felt shame. It was terrible. Then we decide first we have to forgive completely, everybody to everybody, and then we have to build it up respect feeling. Now such a thing can never repeat to us."

His aunt, who had been long silent, spoke up again, shaking a finger at him. She puffed on her cigarette, mashed it out, closed the little box, and went on talking for some time.

Koh sat quietly, looking thoughtful.

"Tell me what she said," I urged.

"She criticize to me, not to you. She said I forget easy so I have to talk this topic tonight. I made you think she might check up if you do anything wrong. It's my mistake. And also, she talked some things about you."

"What did she say?"

"She knows you came here to our country second time. Before that you stay at your grandmother and grandfather. They have a philosophy, too, almost similar to my aunt. She said so. And your mother and father were on the sea, on a boat for a long time. Now they came back, but you don't see them. Just write a letter."

It was true. My parents had purchased a large ketch and had set out with my sisters on an ocean voyage. I had been staying with my grandparents while I was studying in southern California. Throughout my growing years I had listened to my family's philosophical discussions, but while living in my grandparents' home, I had the chance to become directly involved in their thoughts and ideas. My parents had returned after sailing for a year, but by then I was in Seoul. I had not seen them for nearly six years.

"And then she explained about travel. If we go to foreign countries, like you, we try many kinds of food and different custom. In this doing we can know our inside spirit after some time. It is because outside circumstance is changing, changing, and inside spirit keeps the same. She explains us that inside spirit keeps all the time very okay—keeping steady, she said—and outside part is having so much trouble. So body part is outside part, and we have a between part. Any emotion and feelings—any remembering and thinking—this is belonging to between part. Mudang's job is to work for that to help for the people. They try to match it up to inside spirit. So mudang philosophy is about that, she said, and they can understand about the spirit part and the between part."

I found myself watching her as Koh spoke. I was tempted

33

to ask how she knew these things about me—how, in fact, she knew that we were arriving this evening. But I thought better of such a question.

She threw back her head and began to laugh. There was a loud knock. She looked at the door and back at me and went on laughing, shaking her finger at her nephew.

It was contagious and made me feel like laughing, also. I suppressed a chuckle. "What's so funny?" I asked Koh.

"Sometimes she is too much laughing." He looked a bit embarrassed. "It's her habit, I don't know why. I guess she laughs now because she thinks we came here by her idea. She is knowing we will make this philosophy talking. It's funny for her."

There was another knock. She stopped laughing, frowned at the door, and shouted, "Shut up!" Then she grinned at me. Somehow, it struck me funny, and to my embarrassment, I laughed out loud. That started her going again; but in her laughter, she called out, "Open the door!"

Someone stood in the doorway, holding a lighted candle in a glass. "Come on, come on!" Her authoritative tone surprised me. A small boy stepped in, slipping off his shoes. He was wearing a dusty middle school uniform, and his school cap was pulled down over his eyes. For a moment he looked at me in awe, tilting his head so he could see under his visor.

"Speak!" she demanded.

His faint whisper was almost inaudible, but I understood his words: "Grandmother died."

"I know," she said. "Come here, come here!" She held out her arms, and he approached her. She pulled him to her, and taking him in her lap, she removed his cap and hugged his head. "Now she is happy but you are sad. Let's go see."

Again we followed her flashlight beam, walking along behind her in the darkness. The boy ran ahead, and by the time we reached the house, he and an adult—perhaps his father —were waiting at the entrance. They looked serious and composed, but from inside came the loud, mournful wailing of many voices. Koh and I did not go in. Such wakes are not restricted to the immediate family: friends, relatives, and

34

even neighbors often come from near and far and often stay for days to share in the mourning. But Koh and I had discussed this as we walked, and his aunt had agreed. We were not needed there, and the family might be apprehensive at a time like this to have a foreigner in their midst. There would be some ceremony for the departing spirit, and there would be the customary wailing. An indifferent outsider, such as I would surely seem to them, would not be appropriate.

So we sat for a while in the narrow entrance way, among many pairs of Korean shoes and slippers, and waited for Koh's aunt to come out. She had thought she might not be long on this first visit. She could spend a bit more time with us and then return.

Koh attempted to explain to me what would be happening this night. He talked about the mudang's understanding of the step-by-step process of dying and of how the mudang assist both the departing soul and the grieving loved ones to provide for a smooth crossing. But he also affirmed he had little familiarity with these affairs. I realized he wished for me to have an appreciation for his aunt's talents and yet not identify him with all her beliefs.

"But what she does is good," I said. "Don't you think it might be important?"

"Anyway, I suppose you never see such a kind of custom in your country. Even modern people, we don't keep it anymore."

"Well, we do have similar customs, I think. I mean, we have various sorts of funerals and burial ceremonies. And many people do have large gatherings and vigils when someone dies."

"Is it really? We are not thinking so about Westerners. Maybe in Western country you just concern about the dead body, you don't think about the spirit."

"Not always, it depends on the people. But you're right, it was different in the old days. Western people had their old ways, too. The modern ways have some disadvantages, you know. Here so many young people are rushing to be modern, and in my country many young people are beginning to think about the disadvantages. We need villages, I think, or some sort of communities. These customs may be important. You know, in the United States, and maybe even in Seoul, people can just die in their apartments, completely alone. They don't even know their neighbors. In modern societies there are many who have no close friends or family— no one to care for them."

"We are thinking about these things, too. Not just young people—every people. We say the main point of all Asian custom is relation—how do you say? Relationshipping?"

"Relationships."

"No, not just aunt or grandmothers—everyone. The best way of contact between every people. It's relation action."

"I understand," I said. "I know what you're saying." The sound of many loud, wailing voices continued to pour through from the other side of the thin, rice-paper door; it was a strange and unusual background for our conversation about departing souls and human relations. That sound echoes persistently in my memory—in all my recollections of Koh and his aunt.

We left the house and started back down the hill, thinking that Koh's aunt would remain inside much longer than she had expected and that we could visit her another day. But I never saw her again.

As we made our way through the darkness along the downhill path, I wondered again about how she knew the things she told me. How did she know about my grandparents and about my parents' sailing trip? How could she have known what we had talked about on our way to her house? How had she known we were coming? I had felt I ought not ask her; but it occurred to me, as we walked, that I could ask Koh.

"How can I tell you?" Koh responded. "How can I have experience? It belongs to mudang. I told you she has many helping spirits. Maybe they can let her know. Also, you are having your own spirit. She can see it, I think. Maybe she can find it out from yourself."

His conjectures would suffice, I supposed. What other possibilities could there be? So for a while we walked in thought-ful silence.

"You know, for my aunt, mudang is like a job for her. That's her big responsibility. It's almost like army, someway. Like a special army. Once they get in there, they cannot escape their duty." Again he was silent for a long while. "So she have to know, that's all. If she cannot know, how can she be mudang?"

◗ ◗ ◗

All things are interconnected; but for most of us, there are veils and even walls between our various worlds, between ourselves and our surroundings, between one another, even between loved ones. When two lovers sit arm in arm on the mountain and look out over the valley to behold the beauty of the setting sun, one often turns to the other and says with a sense of deep inspiration and longing, "How I wish I could see the world through your eyes!" And, in this setting, they begin to sense that on some level the wish comes true.

At every point of inspiration and experience, with every friend and lover, there is the longing for shared vision—and it is this very longing that pulls lovers the world over to In-spiration Point to watch the sunset, arm in arm. We long for what we know is there. In every realm and region of reality, we share the world and share the view. Even in the realm of the illusion of separateness, we share the view: it is a shared illusion.

We long for what we know is there. Yet, even as we refer to our relatedness, we seem to be immersed in our illusion. The life around us seems to be something "else"—outside and apart—seen only through the switchboards of our sep-arate senses. We agitate between attraction and apprehen-sion. Thus we have the Golden Rule: "Do unto others as you would have others do unto you." It has been said so many ways in so many places over so many centuries. The Golden Rule is the awareness of interrelatedness speaking to the illusion of separateness.

In the realm of the illusion of separateness, we see a myr-

iad of isolated, insulated, skin-encapsulated units—each of whom imagines an "inside" and an "outside." In the realm of the illusion of separateness, we see "myself" and "others." We see adversaries—augmenters of our apprehension. Thus we have the Golden Rule to follow—through the fog of the illusion. How do we relate to pickpockets and thieves? How do we treat those who have mistreated us? The Golden Rule would have us treat all others as we would have all others treat us. Thus will things be put to right and the law of balance restored. Degradation begets delinquency and harm begets harm. Wrongfulness is overcome by righteousness, foolishness by wisdom, cruelty by kindness, and weakness by strength. The Golden Rule is not a lofty aspiration; it is the law. It is the only way things work in balance in this world.

We see our world as we see ourselves, and we see ourselves as our world sees us. People behave in the world as they are seen by others. Images beget actions and actions beget images. Society is the mirror by which the actions and images of everyone reflect onto everyone else. Society is the mirror into which we look for a view of ourselves as we appear to others. "Self-image" and "self-esteem" are the reflections cast upon "self" by society.

The Golden Rule is often set aside when it is needed most, and we forget to "forgive those who have trespassed against us." But the Golden Rule speaks to all and serves in all scenarios; it speaks to victim and villain alike. It does not speak of blame and shame. The pickpocket sees himself as he is seen. If no praise comes to him, he has no praise for himself. He is ashamed. Misfits and malefactors do not care for themselves—and those who do not care for themselves cannot care for others. But those who receive respect reflect respect. We are all, after all, one another. The Golden Rule is the Wisdom of Wholeness calling into the illusion of separateness.

◐   ◐   ◐

I asked my friend how his aunt could know about me—how, in fact, she could know we were coming. It was because she was a mudang. Koh had to struggle to reconcile the different realms of his experience as modernity's promise of material comforts urged him and his people toward a materialistic view. But the mudang was omniscient, and he had witnessed her omniscience. He called her his teacher.

The mudang viewed the world from a different vantage point. From her little hillside home, she could see her neighborhood and all the lights of the city in the distance. She could share the everyday view of those around her; but to her, things could be seen within the context of a larger picture. To the omniscient, all hearts and minds are connected and thus accessible to view. The mudang was a healer. She could look beyond infirmity and injury and see wellness. She knew what all healers know: that wellness is the natural at-balance interrelationship of all things. She could look beyond the outscape of appearance, deception, and illusion and see divinity in everyone.

Not only the injured and the infirm but also the victim— and even the villain—must become the work of the healer. The truly artful and effective healer is able to see, touch, and evoke the point of divinity in the criminal, the point of wellness in the infirm, the point of balance in the seemingly unbalanced.

We all struggle to reconcile the different realms of our existence as modernity's material comforts tend to confine us to a materialistic view. But we all long for the omniscience of the mystic. We long for what we know is there. We go to Inspiration Point that we might catch a fleeting glimpse of what is real—because the illusion keeps coming back. The mudang is omniscient in being a mudang. It comes with the territory. The mudang sits at a superior vantage point. It is the mudang's realm. But the realm of the mudang belongs to everyone; some just don't see it. One who does not know one is a mudang or a mystic is an aspirant. An aspirant aspires to access and to actualize one's own awareness. One who does not know one is an aspirant is an aspirant, nevertheless!

❍   ❍   ❍

I wonder whether the leaves on the tree outside my window have any notion of their existence? Well, they cannot say, "I am a leaf"—not in any sort of language, I suppose. I can only guess that every leaf must on some level (with or without conscious thought) experience its existence. I suppose that is what it means to be alive.

It is fun to watch the rustling leaves and contemplate their experience. I imagine each saying to its own self, "I am a leaf, I am a leaf," and thinking it is quite busy being a leaf who rustles from time to time. If leaves are aware of the other leaves beside them on the branch, they may say, "We are leaves." And if they have any sense of the other branches, they may have developed a sort of "we-they" consciousness, thinking that those "over there" are a different group. Such a "we-they" attitude on the part of the leaves is ridiculous, for it has no meaning for a tree. Still, it seems to promote a sense of fellowship among the leaves on any given branch.

It is difficult to imagine that the leaves have any real appreciation of the total awareness of the tree, who sees itself as a being in its own right. The limited perspective of the leaves has its tragic side: they know they'll die and fall off the branch, and they don't look forward to it.

I cannot help but think that the leaf-experience might be more meaningful and fair if the leaves could be allowed at least a glimpse from time to time of the total tree experience. Perhaps it is so, but as I watch these rustling leaves, I have to wonder how one of them would go about attaining such an experience. Suppose one single little leaf should be still enough and open enough to sense the great consciousness of the larger being as it calls out: "I am a tree!" After all, the consciousness of the tree does indeed flow through—and encompass—every vein of every leaf and root. Yet, how could a leaf hope to enjoy the experience of a tree? There might come some exciting momentary glimpse for the leaf —but then, it would just be a little leaf on a big tree having a personal experience. No matter. A tree is still a tree.

SCENE THREE

Do Not Get Hit

I met Aki (as I'll call him here) on a corner in midtown Manhattan. He had been walking just in front of me, and I had been watching him because I was sure I could tell who he was. I did not know his name yet, or his personal identity, but I could tell who he was. He was wearing a business suit and carrying three small books, which he held in one hand at his side. I could see them clearly: a New York City guidebook, an English-language text (one of those popular generic paperbacks for "the foreign-born" with which I was very familiar), and a plastic-laminated book whose thin pages were edged in shiny gold (the imperative little translation dictionary that Asians everywhere called a "concise").

This was a young businessman from Japan. By his appearance he had quite recently graduated from a fine college, passed all the necessary exams and applications for employment in one of Japan's substantial and growing corporations, and had been assigned a job in the United States. He had been in this country a few months at most and was still at the task of improving his English. My many years in Asia and my close acquaintance with literally dozens of Korean,

41

Chinese, and Japanese students had taught me to recognize who was who. I had become familiar with the lifestyle patterns that Asians so carefully maintain. I could now identify nationality by such subtleties as posture and gait, and this man's dress and his books told me the rest.

When we came to the corner, we both stopped to wait for the traffic signal across the street. I turned to him and spoke. "Where are you from?" I asked.

(It felt reasonable to do this. I had not been in this city much longer than he, I supposed, and having quite recently come from Seoul, I felt rather like a foreigner myself. Besides, I had been spoken to by strangers hundreds of times in the streets and alleys of Japan and Korea. People wanted to practice English. Sometimes youngsters came running from behind hollering, "Wait, wait!" Sometimes students wearing watches would ask me the time. Sometimes people would hope I was lost and, when convinced I was not, would claim they were. Once in an elevator in Seoul, I listened as two shy high school students urged one another in Korean to try some English on me; and I finally told them in their own language that I had already passed my floor to accommodate them and that if one of them didn't eventually talk first, we should be going up and down all day. My inquiry would be appropriate, I felt, from this man's point of view.)

"I am from Japan," he answered.

"I know," I said, "but from where in Japan?"

He named a place I didn't recognize. I told him I had been to Japan several times but knew only Tokyo and Yokohama. This place, he explained, was about midway between those two cities. He had been living in Tokyo for the past several years while attending a university and he had recently been employed by Nissan Motor Company.

When the light changed and we started across, he asked where I was going. We were both walking to the same destination, we discovered—to an international visitors' center a few blocks away—I to rendezvous with a Korean friend and he to seek hotel accommodations.

It was this "coincidence" that led to our immediate acquaintance and our eventual friendship. My Korean friend was late, and Aki and I sat and talked for more than an hour in that center. Since I knew such little Japanese, he attempted to give me some lessons right then. This Aki would never be a typical businessman, I thought. He seemed too quiet, too reserved. There was nothing weak about him, or even shy. He purposefully used a kind of gentleness that I had seen in Asian monks.

I memorized a few new Japanese words, and then Aki decided to chart out the entire Hiragana syllable system so I would have some worthwhile homework. I still have that alphabet written on a napkin. And on the other side is the hotel address which Aki acquired while we were there at the center. That office, it turned out, gave discount certificates for certain New York hotels to certain foreign visitors.

I learned about Aki's situation that day. Soon after his employment at Nissan, Aki had been sent to the United States. He was eventually to be a Datsun engineer representative, but this first year was to be an orientation period. For twelve months he would have few company duties and plenty of time to develop fluency in English and familiarity with American life. He had been here about two months now, and it was not working, he felt. His uncle was a successful businessman with a huge home in Queens, and Aki had been given a room there. He was living with his uncle, his aunt, a few younger cousins, a few servants, and an occasional guest or two, and no one spoke English. It was like being in Japan—the food, the conversation, everything. So he thought that by checking into a hotel, he would get right into the middle of American life.

I wondered what would come of this new arrangement. Aki was provided a room in a transient hotel in the middle of Times Square—a questionable place, I thought, to learn about life in these United States. I promised to keep the napkin, to study Hiragana, and to visit him at his hotel.

More than two weeks passed before I was able to make it to Times Square to call on Aki, and much had happened to him. I got the whole story sitting in the restaurant next to his hotel. Perhaps I was more eager to hear it than he was to tell it. In any case, I questioned persistently and listened patiently until I knew all that had been said and done—by him and to him.

For the first few days Aki had walked up and down the streets trying to strike up a conversation with anyone and everyone. That almost never worked, but whenever it did, he soon had reason to regret it. So Aki tried the old folks who sat in the lobby of his hotel, and he made friends with one old lady who was always knitting.

For the next few days he conversed with this old lady. He heard about her hometown, about how she had moved to New York, and about how her husband had passed away. He could not understand every word, but he was practicing English—and it was company. It was easy to meet her: she was always sitting in the same place and knitting on the same piece. But this, too, soon went wrong. As she inquired about Aki and what he was doing here, she eventually had to hear about Nissan Motors and the Datsun exports. Her response was instant and startling:

"Why, you little monkey!" she cried. "Monkey see, monkey do. Cars were developed in America. We had them from the beginning. The only way you could make cars in Japan is to copy them from us. You people come over here to copy from us and then you try to sell it back to us. No wonder we call you people monkeys."

Aki listened to those remarks and politely excused himself. After that, when he passed her in the lobby, she did not seem to want to talk either. Then there was a young married couple from Pakistan. Aki even visited their room a few times. But they always reverted to their own language, making huge gaps in the conversation for Aki, so that he felt like an empty chair in their room.

One day he noticed, just to the right of the main desk in the lobby, a little sign that said INFORMATION. This, he thought, might be the answer to his problems.

"Please could you tell me—where do you have standard American people?" he asked the man behind the sign. But the man did not understand, and it felt difficult to explain. At last Aki decided what he wanted: "I want to see American families having picnic," he said.

Aki was directed to Central Park, and he set out immediately for another unfortunate adventure. It was close to dusk when he reached Central Park, but he walked about for nearly an hour before deciding he should go back to his hotel and return to the park in the daytime.

Suddenly, there were six men standing in front of him. They seemed to have come from nowhere. "Give us your money!" one shouted. Aki stood quietly. Two men walked around behind him, and one of them gave him a shove. "Give us your money." Aki waited to see what would happen. "Give us your watch!" said another. There was one more shove from behind. Then two men held his arms while another removed his watch, and they were off.

Aki found a policeman just outside the park and decided to say something for the sake of others. He had expected the policeman to be alarmed at this surprising news, but the policeman looked as though this sort of thing happened every day. In fact, he said so.

"It happens every day, every day. You're not from New York here, are you? Well, don't be going in there anymore, you're just asking for trouble when you do. They go in bunches, they get bicycles and everything that way. You come out here after it's too late, what can I do?"

So it was back to the sidewalks of Times Square for Aki. Still not a single American friend came his way. More than once he was approached by someone wanting to sell him a watch. He supposed they were street vendors who had noticed that he didn't have one. Then one young vendor generously explained about "hot" goods, and Aki had an English lesson. Once he thought he saw his own watch, but he said nothing.

I promised Aki I would visit him every day, and I did. We went to restaurants and theaters. We rode boats and subways and elevators and saw the Empire State Building and the Statue of Liberty and all the famous sights. America was looking better now to Aki, and Aki was looking happier to me; but I remembered his having inquired after the whereabouts of the "standard American people."

"Things will get better for you," I told him. "You'll see. In time you'll meet lots of American friends and families. You'll go to picnics and parties and everything." But somehow, I thought, there had to be a change in his situation. His uncle's place had not been ideal, but neither was the hotel at Times Square.

I had a sister and brother-in-law living in Brooklyn; they and their two young children were part of a commune of families. This commune was purchasing a large three-story house on fifty acres in the Catskill Mountains (a property that had been a guest resort for hunters) in order that all the grownups and children could experience a more sharing lifestyle in a more natural setting. I had once been there for a weekend. Soon everyone would be heading up for a three-week stay, and I was invited. This was not exactly a standard situation—or even standard people—but it occurred to me it would be a useful and reassuring experience for Aki.

I consulted with all concerned, got back to Aki, and the matter was arranged. Aki checked out of his hotel (at least temporarily), and we moved into a room under the front porch of this huge New England—style house in the mountains.

This was a charming place, and I supposed Aki had never seen anything like it. The tall wooden house with its gables, porches, and balconies, the long stony walkway that led to the front gate, the wooded hills that rose up behind, the sparkling pond fed by a babbling brook and adorned by a little wooden rainbow bridge, and the ducks waddling on the bright green grass—all these blended together to create a storybook atmosphere that enchanted us all.

People wanted to move up here for good, and part of the purpose in this three-week stay (for all but Aki and me) was to explore how to make the setup work. The place was barely a full day's drive from New York City—easy enough for a stay like this—but it was too far to drive to work and back. The question was how to live in a place like this where the lifestyle seemed so real and yet so unrealistic. Aki and I sometimes listened to the meetings in which people discussed farming, dairying, ranching, cottage crafts and a number of other ideas they thought almost feasible for "achieving freedom" from city and jobs. I explained to Aki that there were a number of groups now exploring communal living, that this was all part of the evolution of a new culture in our country, and that I thought it was good for him to see this—"standard" though it was not.

Aki related best with the kids. There were about ten of them, ranging from six to sixteen, all different in their wants and their ways, and they all competed for Aki's time and attention.

There were four sets of parents, and three other adults: Aki and I—and Bonnie. Bonnie was a very large and busty young woman in her twenties who was either laughing or singing almost every moment. Her laugh was overpowering, but her singing was delightful and engaging. She was a friend of everyone, and she and her guitar were always invited. Aki found her a little scary at first, it seemed to me. Her singing was easy and pleasing to him, but she was a free and hefty hugger, and her loud laugh rang out through the hills and the woods and even made the ducks scatter. This is not seen in Japan. In a manner most pure and natural to herself, she tried to make up for any coldness Aki might have experienced in our country; but to Aki, and by Japanese standards, she was overzealous and almost overwhelming.

Up over the hills to the east, about fifteen minutes' drive on winding dirt roads, there was a pond more than fifty times as large as the one in the yard. In ours you could only dip in and get wet, but in this one you could swim or dive off the rock in the center or lie in the sand under the sun. People called this place the swimming hole, and they came from miles around. It was never crowded because there were never many people miles around.

About eight of us piled into the old pickup one afternoon to take Aki to the swimming hole. It was his first swim since he had left his country, and he appeared to have been missing it, for he was the first to run splashing into the water— with even the swiftest kids trailing behind. Soon he had swum the circumference of the pond and was standing at the shallow end, shaking his head so that shiny drops of water flew through the air.

Suddenly someone shouted from the middle of the pond: "Is that a Jap?"

"What?" I shouted back in an equally loud voice. The sound had simply burst out.

There were two paunchy men in the middle of the pond, sitting on the large rock that people called "the island." With them was an adolescent girl who was likely the daughter of one. The man who had shouted pointed directly at Aki. "Is that there a Japanese?" he shouted again.

I glanced at Aki. He was floating on his back now, looking as though he had not heard. One of the children answered proudly that our friend was indeed from Japan.

"Well, get him out of the swimming hole!" cried the other man in a threatening voice.

Bonnie walked around the edge of the pond and swam up to the rock from the other side, looking as though she were here by herself. "May I come up on the island?" she called in a cheerful voice. Without waiting for a response, she climbed up on the rock and plunked herself down in front of the others. There was barely room for all of them to sit, and Bonnie warmly clasped one man's arm for balance. Then she removed her top and flung it into the water, exposing her large breasts. "The sun is fantastic up here!" said she.

The two men grabbed their adolescent girl, scampered down the rock, splashed to the shore, jumped in their car, and drove off. When the car was out of sight, everyone looked at Bonnie. For a moment she sat atop the rock with her arms folded over her chest, looking both pleased and embarrassed; then she dove into the water and retrieved her top. No more than three or four minutes had passed from the insult to the exit. I thought that was one of the most interesting examples of nonviolent, nonconfrontational offensive defense I had ever seen.

I believe Aki thought so, too. I believe he had really understood the whole affair. He never mentioned it, and none of us recalled the incident in his presence—though it was later discussed because Bonnie wanted the children to know about racism and to hear her reasons for what she called her most unusual behavior. But the next time I saw those two hugging, I knew it had been Aki's idea.

One day Bonnie fell off a bike on the gravel driveway out front, and she seriously injured her head. Some friends who were passing through had driven her and the bike about ten miles up the highway and left her off there to enjoy the exhilarating downhill coast back home. She must have been going thirty miles an hour when she turned onto the gravel drive and hit the front-wheel brake. Aki heard the thump and went running. Her head was pouring blood and we thought she had a concussion. There were no vehicles home at the moment, but this could not wait. I called the dairy farmer who lived a mile down the road, and he came speeding in a cloud of dust. We three piled into his car and headed for the nearest doctor. Aki held a towel around Bonnie's head.

We spent the rest of the day obtaining confirmation that there was no concussion, nothing broken, and nothing out of place—just several deep bruises, painful scratches, and a few open cuts. Bonnie could recuperate at home.

Over the next few days I watched Aki care for Bonnie. He examined her cuts and bruises, cleaned her scalp and face with warm towels, and massaged her neck and shoulders. He held her head against his chest and patted it gently. It was a simple, unassuming friendship these two had found, but I could feel that they had come to share an unusual sort of empathy.

Our days were full, time passed, and Aki was the first to mention one evening that we had but one more day in this place. After dishes, most of the parents and kids left for an overnight trip up north to attend to some business related to the property. Bonnie and I sat in the kitchen and talked about Aki. We wondered what might come of his life in our country over the months and years ahead. We wondered what he would do now upon returning to the city. We felt it unlikely he would ever be back, and Bonnie wondered where, when, or whether she might ever see him again.

We decided to play a trick on Aki. How that thought arose

I'm sure neither of us could say, but somehow we decided to play a trick, and we spent a long time arriving at the perfect idea. It was to be the dumping pail trick. Quickly—before Aki should come wandering up from his room downstairs—we braced a board across a two-foot gap from the slightly open side door to the molding and balanced a nearly full bucket of water atop the board so that it would fall on Aki when he came through the door.

Perhaps we thought this yet another example of life in America—a trick unheard of in Japan, no doubt—something Aki could take back with him in his bag of memories. In any case, it was fun setting up our trick, and Bonnie was giggling with anticipation as she sent me downstairs to fetch Aki.

As I entered the room, I saw him standing at the mirror before a pan of water. "Why are you shaving in here?" I asked. "In fact, why are you shaving at this time of night?"

"I need it," he answered. "This is every man's have-to-do thing."

"Well, anyway, Bonnie wants to see you. She asked me to get you."

"Okay, good!" Aki laughed. "Now we know my shaving reason. I better use this." From his pack he pulled a small bottle with a Japanese label. It was either aftershave or cologne. He splashed a few aromatic drops on his cheeks. "Let's go. I'm ready."

We ascended the steps to the side porch, and I glanced through the slightly open door. I almost started laughing. Bonnie had planted herself upon a folding chair squarely in front of the upcoming scene, and I knew there was a stifled whoop behind the hand she held over her face. Then I realized a need for instant strategy: As I was slightly older than my Japanese friend, he was always last in every one-at-a-time situation. Now he had to walk in before me. I stopped as though to tie my shoe and motioned him on. Bonnie managed a squeaky, "Aki, come here," holding back a give-away laugh.

In a moment it was over. Aki stood in the doorway, drenched. The bucket had dumped itself right on target and rolled across the floor. Bonnie held tight to the seat of her chair and whooped with such ferocious delight that the whole chair rocked and the very house seemed to shake. Aki looked shocked and very ashamed. He stood motionless for a long moment, his clothes dripping. Then he shook his head slightly and mumbled very quietly, "No good."

I felt a rush of guilt. Why had we done this cruel and puzzling thing to this gentle foreign friend? I could not think of anything to say. Bonnie also felt it. Her expression changed from glee to pain, and she stood up to hug him.

To my relief, Aki suddenly laughed. "No, no, no. No wet hugging. If you need water, you get your own. I help you. And no wet hugging. Wet hugging is too much liberal." He went downstairs to change his clothes.

Bonnie and I cleaned up our mess. "What do you suppose he thinks of us now?" she asked. I told her I was not sure, and beyond those words, we were silent.

When I went down to join Aki, I found the words to apologize. "We should not have done that," I admitted. "I guess we thought it would be another experience for you, but it was stupid and I'm sorry."

"That was not good," said Aki, "really not good. I hope you try again."

For a moment I was puzzled. Did he mean my apology was insufficient and I should try it again?

But he went on. "Next time you please try something different. Same thing again is too easy. You try anything you want. Maybe you throw something at my back. Now I know I am no good in these days. In America I lost everything."

"What are you talking about?"

"I make mistake. You saw me. I got wet!"

"But Aki, it was a trick. That's what's supposed to happen when—"

"Yeah, trick. I understand trick. But I missed. I should catch it."

"You could never catch it, Aki. A tipping bucket full of water? You could never catch it. It's not your fault. It's our fault—we shouldn't have done it."

51

"Fault? Nobody fault. Only me. This is my training. You don't know. First mistake, I feel nothing, so I got in the door. Second mistake, I do nothing, so I got wet. I am not quick. I lost all my speed. No good." He shook his head again. "If my teacher would see . . . " He stopped himself.

I watched him for a moment. It began to come together. I had met a couple martial artists in Asia—genuine adepts. They were extremely quiet and gentle people. They were like Aki. They too could nearly fly. Now it fit. I recalled the scene from several days earlier—the scene I had dismissed as a mistaken impression. I was sitting in the living room talking to one of the mothers while Aki was playing with the children outside. All afternoon he had been teaching them a kind of tumbling, and we could hear their happy cheers and laughter. I was facing the window that looked over the porch; and once, for a fleeting second, I thought I saw Aki fly past that window as though he had leapt as high as the eaves of the porch roof. It was unlikely: this main floor was two stories up from ground level. Laura was facing me and she simply went on talking. I decided I had not really seen this, and I went on listening.

"What training?" I asked. "What teacher?"

Aki said nothing. He stood up and quietly walked outside. I waited a moment to follow. I wanted to be thoughtful, but I wanted to pursue this. We sat by the little bridge that went over the brook. The bubbling water and the singing crickets made a pleasant sound. Then it started slowly and went on a long while: Aki talked as he had never talked before.

This gentle friend had black belts in judo, karate, and aikido, and was an adept of the highest degree in a few other disciplines whose names were barely familiar. He had been a student of martial arts from childhood. His life had been devoted to strict and steady discipline.

At one point in our conversation, I suddenly remembered Aki's episode in Central Park. "Wait a minute," I blurted out. "What about that watch? How come you lost your watch in Central Park that day?"

"There were six," he answered simply. "Six is too many."

"Now wait a minute," I went on. "I've watched a few martial arts movies, man. I've seen one single guy—"

Aki put his fingers over my lips and prevented me from going on. It seemed an unusual gesture for Aki. He sat there with his hand on my face, staring at me quietly as though my understanding might come better through the silence. But after a moment, he allowed me my explanation. He literally whispered, and I had to strain to hear him. It had a powerful effect on me. For the first time since I met him, I was now fully aware of Aki's immense strength and composure. For the first time, I felt myself look up to him.

"Those movies have no sense. No truth, no teaching. It is not this way. The training is not for fighting. It is not for protection of myself. There is no myself. Myself is yourself. It is the same. I can keep my watch—but if I keep my watch, this is self-protection. In America you want this training for self-protection. This is big misunderstanding. What is to protect? One watch? This is nonsense!

"If I save my watch, what happens? I must knock down many man. They cannot get up again soon. I have training to do this. But first I have training for judgment. Then I practice control to keep the judgment first. What is better, one watch or one tooth of human being? Tooth is better. This is the judgment. Compared to any human part, the watch must be less value.

"I should feel six man before they come to me. It was my mistake. I forgot my training. That's what I told you about your trick. My mistake. I should feel intention before it comes to happening. But if I hurt six man—even three man —to correction my mistake, my training is useless. I am just a bad man who have nice watch."

We sat and listened to the crickets and the brook. These sounds seemed loud to me now after having strained to his whispers. "What you say feels right to me," I said, working to keep my voice as calm as his. "But it is not the usual judgment—not the usual sense of values that we find in my country, not even for people who take training."

DO NOT GET HIT

"It is also in my country now. Bad boys study karate for playing fighting in the street. It is all becoming changed."

Aki had attended a very special school. It was one of the only truly traditional training centers remaining in his country (and unlike anything in the United States, to the best of my knowledge). Aki and his fellow trainees had entered their dojo as children. It was not easy to get in. They and their parents had to pass interviews and tests. And then for years they received only philosophy and strenuous disciplines for self-control. There was no sparring for them. There were no flips and falls. They had been prepared to expect this. They had been told that if they wanted to learn fighting, there were countless dojos whose only requirement for entry was the payment of tuition. And this had been made emphatically clear on the first day when the highest instructor, the one Aki called Karate Master, gave the orientation.

Each time a new group of beginners formed, Aki told me, the karate master would gather the youngsters at his feet. He would stand towering above them, looking stern, and he would explain that for four years they would practice mental and emotional disciplines. For four years they would learn self-control—four years before they would try any of the physical tricks and tactics that other dojos offered on the very first day. If any of them disapproved of this idea, they were requested to leave now, before the instructors should waste even an hour's time on them.

"Nobody ever wanted to leave," Aki said. "In many years we saw so many new students coming. It was so difficult, but nobody wanted to leave. Sometimes they were put out by Karate Master's deciding."

The karate master cautioned the new pupils that this first four years was a test period. Every day was to be a test—both inside and outside the dojo. They were to maintain good health, attend school regularly, get good marks, and above all, they were not to fight—not at school or at home or at play or ever.

"If you should ever fight," this teacher had said, "ever even once during these four years, you can change to another dojo. You cannot continue here."

54

This last admonition had caused a stir in Aki's group (as he supposed was the case with every new class), and the children began talking among themselves.

"What if someone starts a fight with us?" one youngster asked.

"Yeah, some kids are always starting trouble," another added.

"Well, just don't hit first," someone offered.

And another: "Right. We should just explain that we're not supposed to fight."

And someone said something like, "Turn the other cheek."

Then suddenly they felt the master's sharp gaze, and they fell silent, realizing they had been chattering among themselves while he watched.

"You do not sense my meaning, so you discuss it among yourselves? How useless! Why do you not ask the one who said this? Am I not still here?"

They waited.

"Well, ask me!"

"What do you mean?" someone asked meekly.

"What do I mean by what?"

"What do you mean by saying, 'Do not fight'?"

"I mean," said the teacher, pausing for effect and speaking slowly, "Do not get hit! If you get hit, you fail!"

Aki assured me that his master had explained there was no blame or shame in such failure. He knew that he was testing his young aspirants from the first day on a principle he would need four years to teach. "Something may happen to you which you will think is not your fault. You will blame someone. But I will blame no one. This is because I understand how things happen. Or, you will call it chance. But I will call it your doing. This is because I have great admiration for you. I understand and respect your capacity for self-control. My expectations for you come out of this respect. Perhaps, if you can feel my respect, it will help you on your way."

Aki watched me for a moment as if to see if I were following. After years of communicating across a whole spectrum of "broken English," I was able to fill in the spaces as I listened now to this friend. I could hear what was in his mind to say. I had been listening, in fact, to the karate master. I was following. Aki picked up a stone from beside the stream and held it up for me to see. "If I want this stone, I pick it up. If I do not want, I do not pick it up. This kind of deciding is easy. It is outside deciding. I don't know how you say it. There are two kinds of deciding—outside and inside.

"The training is the outside mind to understand the inside deciding. If mastering this, all things are controlled by knowing and deciding. If it is my alone mind, or if it is our together mind, still all things are depending on mind's deciding. If really we want to control it, we have to bring it to the outside knowing. I cannot explain in English. It is difficult even in my language. Anyway, if somebody hits me, it must have been decided also by myself."

Again we were silent. For a long time we listened to the night sounds. Aki seemed to feel that enough had been said. I put my hand in the stream and felt the current pushing against my palm. Images of Aki passed through my mind. I pictured him in Central Park, in the hotel lobby, in the swimming hole, and standing in that doorway dripping wet. I tried to picture him in his own country. I tried to see him training in his dojo.

The one who hits and the one who gets hit are together in that arrangement, I thought to myself. Together, on that inside level, they co-create the scenario that is then projected on the outside. These things have been said many times over the centuries. But it felt interesting to realize that I was sitting by a young contemporary who worked for Nissan, yet who had also been trained to experience this reality. He had lost his watch in Central Park and called it his mistake. Perhaps if this had happened to an ordinary black belt, someone might have been hurt. The fact that no one was hurt was unusual enough, I thought, but the personal attitude Aki had developed was almost unheard of—at least in our contemporary culture.

And there was another thing. When we had sat in that restaurant near his hotel and he had recounted the episode in Central Park, I had felt sympathy for him. He seemed a soft and mild person. I had not known he was capable of protecting either his watch or himself. It had never occurred to Aki to care whether I knew it or not. It had never occurred to him to say, "If I had wanted to, I could have . . . "

Now, as I watched him sitting quietly by the stream, I appreciated knowing what he could have done. I had always been aware of his mild manners and his gentle politeness, and now I appreciated knowing something of both his strength and his wisdom. "Why did you come to the United States?" I asked. "What are you going to do with the automobile industry?" He did not seem like a businessman to me. He did not fit the usual image of a martial arts expert either, but the life that seemed most likely for him here in America could hardly be what he had trained for.

"It is for my job," he answered. "I took university training for my job and company training for my job. But it is not my real training. My real training is for my life—for my real life." We returned to our room. Aki selected one of his cassettes for the tape deck, and we listened to music. We never talked on that subject again.

I was able to meet with Aki only a few times after we got back to the city. For some reason he returned to Japan earlier than expected. I got a brief note just saying hello. It would be fun to find him again someday, standing at the curb in some other corner of the world—waiting for the light to change.

◐   ◐   ◐

A person who gets hit is involved in an unfolding sequence —a scenario—in which the moment of contact is neither the beginning nor the end. Both "hitter" and "hittee" create the scenario.

Do not get hit.*"* *This is easier said than done—or not done, as the case may be. Most everything, especially anything that is not easy, requires a measure of ability, and ability requires training. Imagine learning not to get hit. How does one practice that?*

One practices one's posture—one's mental-emotional

57

posture. The first step in Aki's training was attitude control. Before Aki and his young classmates could begin to practice their physical stances, they had to practice their mental-emotional stances. When Aki talked about his episode in Central Park, I was struck by his eminent attitude. It was his unique emotional control that was his special strength, and this strength was apparent in his very nature. But he had practiced it for years. He had learned to be attentive to his attitudes and to the circumstances they created. Attitudes radiate, and subtle or subliminal though they may be, they invariably invoke response.

Attitude is one thing; but once a scenario is set in motion, how would attitude stop a bullet or a punch? One must anticipate. Anticipation develops even with physical training: one learns to anticipate the coming blows and throws even before the movements are initiated, just as the mongoose, locked onto the eyes of the cobra, detects the lightning movements before they happen.

But how does one anticipate the path of an approaching potential thief—or a bucket of water invisibly poised and ready to fall? The ancient concept of nonattachment that still endures in many traditions and philosophies around the world is that one is not one's body and therefore not the attractions and reactions that it seems to be caught up in. It is the concept that one can move one's vantage point to outside of one's affairs and thus achieve a wider view—a view from which one "sees" the bucket and anticipates the fall.

Among one native people there was this dictum, attributed to a village prophet: "Should any of you think yourself in conflict or contention, then find the highest tree and climb it." Escape? "Fight or flight," if you take it literally. But one could "climb a tree" with one's perspective and look down on one's predicament from the highest possible point. One could look down on one's own self, so to speak, from aloft and aloof. To attain such a vantage point would enhance attitude because one could observe and adjust one's relative position. To maintain such a vantage point would enhance anticipation, because one would always see what is coming.

The body is on the ground, but the mind is on the ground and in the tree as well. Not all of the mind is in the body. The higher vantage point does exist, and the view is seen. It is a matter of making the wider view known to the body in order for, as Aki put it, "the outside mind to understand the inside deciding . . . to bring it to the outside knowing." This is possible with training, since all of the body is in the mind.

● ● ●

"All of the body is in the mind. Not all of the mind is in the body, but all of the body is in the mind." Swami Rama used to say that.

Many times I thought of Aki when Swami said time and again, "Strength is a gentle thing." He would say it when he would find an opportunity to admonish some young person for bragging about his strength or toughness. But on occasion, he seemed to show off a bit himself, suddenly lifting some startled adult person up over his head, or snapping a pencil, or twisting a metal ruler with a graceful wave of his wrist and a flick of his finger. But then, again, he would say, "Do you not know what is strength? Strength is a gentle thing."

To the Swami, strength was mind power playing out in the physical realm. To him, strength was an aesthetic thing. It was an art. It involved will and skill but had nothing to do with violence or confrontation—or even a sense of defense. To Swami Rama—and to the yogis and the adepts—strength is a matter of self-mastery, nothing more, nothing less.

So it was the concept of self-mastery that was presented in the first four years of Aki's training, before he could start with his physical training—the throws and tumbles that other dojos took from the beginning. More than four years, it seems, would likely be required to develop and perfect it —more than a lifetime, perhaps. But it was as useful as it was exceptional, in Aki's view, to begin with and to build upon the concept of self-mastery rather than the notion of self-defense.

Such special schools do still exist—in nearly secluded temples in the Diamond Mountains of Korea, for example—

59

where martial arts training consists essentially of dissolving one's illusory sense of self. But the essential aspects of the ancient forms of martial arts, we are told, were long ago taken aside, made secret, and kept carefully guarded, away from the general population. Without careful protection from general use, such training and such powerful techniques— and their benevolent application—could not have safely survived the tumultuous transitions that occurred throughout the Orient. Yet, while such sequestering may have served to safeguard the esoteric teachings, it may also have served to adulterate the popular conception and consumption of martial arts training.

Today, in both East and West, martial arts training becomes little more than the superficial remnants of the ancient arts. Now martial arts is usually presented commercially, often in a concise or cursory format, and actually advertised for "self-defense," while teachers, as well as aspirants, often lose sight of the true philosophical and spiritual connections and implications.

It is not self-defense but self-mastery that the adepts have learned. To maintain and assert the illusory sense of a separate, contending self, to encourage and nourish a preoccupation with adversity and defensiveness—this is precisely what martial arts is not. Self-mastery involves developing a concept of self quite different from the contemporary meaning implied when using the English words "self" and "defense." Self-mastery involves overcoming the illusion of the isolated self.

This basic principle of self-mastery must be what Aki's karate master had in mind when he told his new students, "Do not get hit." Aki's style and philosophy seemed to suggest a sense of a collective self—of an interplay between mutual and individual will and intent. Because of the interrelatedness of all things, each "self" is a responsible participant in the collective will of all of life. One way of saying this is that both "hitter" and "hittee" are co-creators of the scenario in which someone hits someone.

Such a thought threatens those who prefer to hold onto a

60

we-they, victim-consciousness point of view. But a we-they point of view is threatening in itself. It will be a co-creation philosophy, rather than a self-defense philosophy, that will provide workable solutions for our contemporary social problems.

Six thieves robbed an expert fighter in Central Park—but there were no injuries. This required superior strength. Superior strength minimizes the damage. No one was hit.

The very idea of defense assumes an image of weakness. Defensiveness sustains divisiveness and divisiveness sustains fear. Strength is a gentle thing. The notion of conquest is born of fear. Even the fearful fantasy of man conquering nature must give way, at last, to the awareness that humankind belongs to nature. Nature is not foe but family, and victory is found in harmony. Strength is a gentle thing. Strength obliterates the illusion of an adversary.

The illusion of the adversary is already being transcended. As the environmental crisis grows, so does the sense of mutual responsibility and the move toward collective measures on a planetary scale. As planetary consciousness grows, nations grow together in their common needs and hopes, and the we-they illusion fades. Now many of us are finding the gentle strength to name our aims and aspirations in terms of what we are striving for rather than struggling against. Though many now sense that fighting wars against nations will not bring peace, they still believe that waging "war" on cancer and waging "war" on drugs might somehow bring health. But many others are now imagining the co-creation scenarios of peace and health in which no one gets hit.

It appears, in any case, that we are not nearly done with the most pertinent of life's lessons—not most of us, at any rate—not in this lifetime. No doubt all of Aki's karate classmates, now much older and wiser (and many of them, no doubt, quite highly trained), are still working with the ideas that the karate master presented in orientation class on that first day—and so, perhaps, is the karate master.

SCENE FOUR

The Soft Body

After having lived and worked with Rolling Thunder, the traditional American Indian medicine man, I moved from his town of Carlin, Nevada, to the San Francisco Bay Area and began my work on the book about him. I and five Japanese roommates rented a large flat in the East Bay, across the bridge from San Francisco. It had several bedrooms, a living room, and a sort of Japanese den, and a little room that I could use for a writing studio. Tsutomu Hayashi and I had been renting a small apartment with his brother Kozo ever since Tsutomu had gone with me to Carlin to visit Rolling Thunder. Tsutomu had become intrigued with the possibilities for adventure and had extended his stay, leaving Kozo to return alone to their family in Sakai.

Even as Kozo was preparing to leave, I had assured Tsutomu that I would welcome any one of his Japanese friends to stay with us—because I knew he needed a companion with whom he could speak his own language in his own home. Tsutomu then found not one but four friends, all of whom wanted to join us; so we had to move to a place large enough for the six of us.

As soon as we were settled into our new Japanese household, it became apparent that evening conversation time was expected to be part of the arrangement. It was a challenge for me because my five roommates differed greatly in English ability. For the first several evenings, every one of them made sure he was there in the living room for evening conversation time. Mostly they wanted me to do the work while they sat and listened. It seemed to go smoothly enough, because those who could not follow me easily pretended to understand and were filled in later by the others.

"How do you meet Tsutomu at first time?" someone asked one evening as soon as we had all gathered in the living room.

"It was on the street in San Francisco," I recalled. "Just a few blocks from the Chinatown Gate." Tsutomu nodded his head in agreement, but when I mentioned that he had been lost and unable to find his way home, he wanted to change the subject. "Tsutomu and his brother were staying with some friends in San Francisco," I went on, "and Tsutomu had gone out for a pack of cigarettes and forgotten the way back."

"Because he was just newly to States," his friend interjected.

"Right, it's easy to get lost in a new place. Fortunately he had the address written down, so I took him to where he was staying and I met Kozo and his friends."

"And then you took Tsutomu to see Rolling Thunder, right?"

"Well, that was a couple of weeks later. I had just finished spending a lot of time with Rolling Thunder, and I told Kozo and Tsutomu about him. Tsutomu became really interested, so when I made a trip back to Carlin, I took him with me."

"That time Rolling Thunder chased away those guys. Tsutomu saw that."

I knew that Tsutomu had told our roommates about the time when Rolling Thunder had chased away some intruders. Now they wanted me to repeat the story.

"But you already know about that, Tsutomu told you all about it. Why would you want to hear it again?"

63

"Now we hear from you in English," was the reply. "Anyway, this is English time."

"Well, Tsutomu and I took the train from Oakland and spent a week out in Carlin," I began. "During that time Rolling Thunder had to go out on a job for the railroad for a few days, so we just hung out in Carlin. On the day he was supposed to return, his train was late getting in, so we sat in his living room and waited. Spotted Fawn had cooked a delicious dinner, and we were really hungry smelling that food. But we had to wait. Since Rolling Thunder was expected, no one could eat ahead of him—"

"They just want to hear about those prowlers," Tsutomu interrupted.

"Well, I'm getting to that," I told him. He was right, they did not need to know the circumstances—and not all of them could follow me anyway. They just wanted to hear about Rolling Thunder's shouting and frightening the prowlers. So I showed them how Rolling Thunder had sniffed the air the moment he came in through the door and put down his brakeman's lantern. Somehow, he had sensed that something was wrong—that someone was nearby who didn't belong.

I stood up and gestured as though I were Rolling Thunder, trying to make the picture clear to them. I walked to the imaginary door and looked out, sniffing the air, and I called to Spotted Eagle as Rolling Thunder had done. I showed them how Rolling Thunder had stepped out to the front of the house and "sensed" the presence of the prowlers some hundred yards or more away. They were in his special storage shed that was part of his own private space across the street. "I was standing like this," I explained, "right behind Rolling Thunder. And Spotted Eagle started across the street, like this, going way around this way, and Tsutomu was standing in the doorway, right behind me. And Rolling Thunder just stood there—so still . . . "

I allowed a long silence, just as it had happened, recalling how Rolling Thunder had stood like a shadow, peering into the darkness, and had then let out that bloodcurdling howl. Suddenly, and to my own surprise, I made that very sound.

64

It came up from my stomach and out of my mouth, filling our living room, shaking the walls, and ringing in the air. I felt an electric shock in the back of my head, just as it had happened to me that night in Carlin. Everyone was startled. Never before had I produced such a sound. For a moment there was a buzzing in my head, and my Japanese friends just stared at me. But I recovered and went on with the story, telling how two dark silhouettes had come running out of the shed and how one of them had come right toward me and then turned to escape across the road. "Spotted Eagle tried to chase one of them but he came walking back, completely out of breath, and he said that that he couldn't get a good look at them, in the darkness . . . " But my friends just sat and stared at me.

So I sat down. I had tried to supplement my English words with drama, and perhaps I had overdone it. I felt strange. No one spoke, and I thought perhaps I should go on talking. Just then the phone rang.

It was Rolling Thunder. I had not seen or heard from him in weeks. "Did you call me?" he asked. For a long while, I said nothing, and he repeated his question. "Did you want me? Are you all right?"

"No," I blurted. "I mean, I didn't call you. I'm fine. I mean, we were just talking about you. I wasn't trying to—"

"I just thought I'd check how you're getting along," he interrupted calmly. "I thought maybe you wanted to talk to me. I was in the car, so I pulled over to a pay phone just now. We're all doin' good up our way. So I guess I'll be goin' on. We can talk later."

"That was Rolling Thunder," I said. Our friends were almost disbelieving, but Tsutomu enjoyed it thoroughly, laughing out loud.

Tsutomu had another Japanese friend in San Francisco. This friend and his American wife had also come to know Rolling Thunder, and they had accommodated him in their home several times when he was in the Bay Area. This friend phoned us one day and asked us to meet them. They had a new guest from Japan whom they wanted us to see, and they invited us to join them for a picnic in the park. We rendez-voused just outside the gateway to the Japanese Garden in San Francisco's Golden Gate Park, and our friends intro-duced us to Takahashi San.

Tsutomu's friend had described their Japanese guest on the phone when he had called. In fact, it was partly owing to this description that we two had agreed to take the bus across the bay on such short notice. This man was indeed—at least to all appearances—an authentic samurai out of Ja-pan's traditional past, and I was glad I had been somewhat prepared before seeing him. He had the traditional topknot in his hair and wooden clogs on his feet. He wore the samu-rai's kimono, complete with all the accoutrements, including two authentic samurai swords at his waist.

The Japanese Garden always had a good number of Asian sightseers strolling along the paths over the little rainbow bridges, and these Asians, much more so than the Western-ers, stared pointedly at Takahashi San. We found a little patch of grass where we could stretch out, away from the Sunday tourist traffic, and there we had our picnic lunch.

This man spoke not a word of English, and though Tsu-tomu and his friend translated bits and pieces for me from time to time, I knew I was missing the essence of whatever was being said. I did learn that Takahashi was serious about his costume. He had learned and lived, to the best of his individual capacity, the true philosophy and art of the sam-urai, and he had come to the United States to set to rights the misconceptions about the samurai that he felt were prev-alent in the West. At first he seemed elated to be in these gardens where a variety of traditional Japanese structures and artifacts provided the ideal symbolism to illustrate his philosophical discourse. But our stay was spoiled as he began to attract more attention. People stopped to stare at him and pointed him out to others who happened by until there was a small crowd of spectators.

Takahashi San was somewhat used to this, I was told, as we started back to the car, and it was partly for my sake that they had decided to leave. He had not wanted me to see all those looks of embarrassed disapproval on the faces of his own people.

"You have it easier in some ways," he said to me as his Japanese host translated, "easier in some ways than I do." I was sitting next to him in the back seat of the car as the five of us rode back to their house. He looked straight ahead as he spoke, pausing to allow for the translation. "I know something about your way. You want to see every kind of style. You travel here and there and try to remain changeable. You just try to fit in. I have to go around like this. It looks like I'm crazy. If I listen to my ego, I should give it up. Sometimes it is too hard for me, but it is my duty in this world."

I did not think he was crazy, but he had certainly chosen a strange line of work. Tsutomu seemed to be impressed with him. We sat on mats in his friends' living room, and Tsutomu listened intently. Tsutomu was not attracted to pretense or show. I knew that he had often spent time at the Zen Center in San Francisco and that he had quietly maintained his own meditation practice without feeling a need to discuss it with anyone. As I watched him listening to Takahashi San, I hoped he would later be able to convey to me the essence of his words. But then I decided that this meeting was more for Tsutomu than for me, and I retired to my own thoughts.

I sat patiently for more than two hours before I began to get restless. I had made other plans for the evening and now I was late, but still I felt hesitant to urge Tsutomu away. I had gotten a slight headache sitting on the grass in the park, squinting into the sun, and now it was beginning to bother me. I looked behind me for a cushion, wondering if it would be all right for me to lie back. I had sat with them so long without understanding anything at all.

Takahashi reached past Tsutomu and took hold of my hand, pulling me toward him. It seemed that he had sensed my discomfort, and I was more than willing to receive whatever help he could offer. But he only sat gazing at my open hand. He took my other hand and held them both, turning them front and back as though to examine them. I really hoped he was not planning to read my palm. I was not in the mood to have my fortune told, even if it meant experiencing some obscure aspect of the samurai tradition. When he began to examine my wrists, and then my forearms and upper arms, one arm at a time, I knew this was not palm reading. He looked at my shoulders and the back of my neck and checked my eyes and my forehead, and I began to wonder what he was expecting to discover.

He considered me contemplatively, occasionally giving me a very gentle poke. If he was preparing to offer some shiatsu or massage, I thought to myself, I wanted him to begin. I had had enough of his checking me over. Then my headache disappeared. I began to feel extremely comfortable. I looked down at my left arm, which was resting on his knee, and realized I could not feel it. I could not feel his hands on me, and I knew he was touching me. There was no sensation in my body. Yet I was not numb, I was energized. It was as though I had come alive—more alive than I had been in a long time. I supposed that I was out of my body—or partway out—and that he had done this to me. But I felt comfortable and totally at ease.

Takahashi spoke to Tsutomu, several times gesturing at me. "He says thanks to you to visit to him," Tsutomu translated. "And apologize to you that he couldn't have any chances to learn English yet. So we have to go out now and maybe we meet again next chance."

Takahashi stood up and bowed, and Tsutomu quickly followed. That brought me to my feet. I could not have been out of my body, I decided, and if I had lost sensation, I had regained it. I touched one hand with the other to confirm that I could feel.

"Also he told that your condition is good. Every people gets off of balance in that part—how do you call it? Maybe electric is going more to one side or the other. It's a usual thing—not relation for just today. Now it's increased, right? More opened up. Can I call it electricity?"

He turned to his friend for help, and they conversed for a moment in Japanese. Takahashi laughed as he listened, but said nothing. They were considering various English words, trying to find an appropriate explanation, and Takahashi could not assist with that.

"Current!" the friend said to me. "It means current, I think, because it has motion. We don't explain because we don't know exactly."

I pursued the matter with Tsutomu as we walked along the steep San Francisco sidewalk back toward the Powell Street cable car. I was still feeling as though I had received some sort of tune-up. It might have been a placebo effect, but I'd had no idea that anything at all was being done to me until it was over. "Were you watching?" I asked. "Did you see what Takahashi San was doing?"

"I watched, but I couldn't see completely. Only he could see it."

"What do you think he could see that you couldn't?"

"Because, if we look at this body, it looks like meat, right? We think we are such a material. But it's made by electricity power. You say current? Takahashi San can touch to your current by his own current. Anyway, we can't explain in English."

"You explained it all right," I said. "In fact, I like your explanation."

"Even in our own language we don't understand it much, so we listen to such a people like Takahashi San."

"But does all this have anything to do with samurai? Do you think he's really a samurai?"

"I don't know why he keeps that style. But he has really big knowledge. Maybe in samurai time the people had such knowledge, and in modern time most of people just forget about it."

Tsutomu and I did see Takahashi once again, some weeks later. It was a chance encounter. We were standing in front of a Berkeley restaurant where I was using the pay phone. We had decided to drop in on one of my sisters, who lived about a mile from where we were, and I was calling to confirm that she was home before setting out on foot. I had just dialed the number when Tsutomu exclaimed, "It's Takahashi San!" There he was on the next block above us, walking along the street in his usual samurai regalia, and there were a half-dozen young people, all Japanese, following along behind, single file, like a row of ducklings.

Tsutomu made a dash to catch up, and I knew he was going to follow.

"Hello?" said the voice on the phone.

"Never mind, I'll call you back," I said, and I ran to join them, not knowing where we were going.

Takahashi San did not know where he was going either, but the young man next in line was giving verbal directions from behind as we walked along single file. In the middle of the next block, Takahashi turned left as instructed, and we started up the sidewalk toward the front porch. A middle-aged man stepped out on the porch to greet us and invite us in. He had shoulder-length, reddish-brown hair and a beard and rimless glasses that were nearly square. I thought he looked familiar.

As soon as we were inside and introductions were made, he recognized me. He had met me some months before at an event with Rolling Thunder. Someone brought out tea for all of us, and our host asked me to join him at his table and proceeded to engage me in a conversation about Rolling Thunder. He and a number of other healthcare professionals were planning a networking trip to China, he told me, to observe and record the practice of acupuncture in that country. He thought it would be great if Rolling Thunder could be a part of that group, and he wondered if I could help him arrange it.

As we talked, I tried to watch Takahashi out of the corner of my eye. He was working on a young Japanese girl who looked about college age. She had been here when we arrived, and she was the reason Takahashi had come. He had been here before, I learned, to assist several people our host had met at the clinic where he worked—all Japanese friends of his who were acquainted with one another and quite receptive to this arrangement. Remembering how he had worked on me and how it had affected me, I wanted to see this procedure. But it was difficult to watch and to talk about China and acupuncture and Rolling Thunder at the same time. In any case, Takahashi was going on for a very long

time, massaging the air around his subject's shoulders—
only occasionally touching her, it seemed, and then only
very slightly. That was all there was to see.

We continued our conversation, and I had another cup of
tea, and all the people on the floor behind me were so quiet
it was easy to forget that they were there. So when Takahashi
let out a yell and the girl screamed loudly, it was extremely
startling. I turned around in time to see Takahashi holding
his sword with two hands just above her shoulder. Instantly
she scrambled across the carpet on all fours, pushing herself
against the wall in the farthest corner and looking quite
frightened. I could feel my own skin tingling from the sound
of his yell and her scream. She must have been terrified. It
must have seemed to her that he was about to chop her head
off.

Takahashi looked disappointed. His entire entourage
looked disappointed, and they admonished her in Japanese.
They seemed to be telling her that she ought not to have
moved. Takahashi replaced his sword in its sheath at his
side, called out a name, and pointed to the floor at his feet.
One young man crawled up to sit in front of him just as the
girl had been sitting. At Takahashi's instructions, he pulled
off his T-shirt, rolled it up, and held it in his lap. He sat with
his eyes closed, absolutely straight and motionless. We all
watched intently now as Takahashi began to work around his
shoulders. Again he went on for a long time, working so
slowly and gently that after twenty or thirty minutes it became difficult to remain attentive.

Now people began to whisper, and our host quietly continued with his ongoing description of his China plans and his
past experiences. I sipped my tea and ate cookies, and when
Takahashi yelled, I was again facing the wrong way. This
time there was no scream. Out of the corner of my eye, I saw
Takahashi jump, swinging his sword through the air, stepping forward on one foot and bending his knees. By the time
I could see clearly what was happening, Takahashi was holding his sword tightly with both hands just above this young
man's shoulder. His shoulder was split wide open and there
was a huge, bleeding gash. His arm was about to fall off on

the carpet. I felt a rush of nausea and a lump in my throat. Everyone was stark still—including, I realized, the demonstrator himself. The young man remained motionless with his eyes closed and a calm expression on his face.

Perhaps he had not actually been injured after all. At least he was feeling no pain. I blinked and shook my head and tried to see more clearly. The bright red band looked like a crimson ribbon that had been placed over his shoulder. But it was not a ribbon. If it was blood, it was under the skin, for it was not running. The young lady for whose benefit this demonstration had occurred was asked to come forward and put her hand on his shoulder. This, apparently, was what was supposed to have happened to her. She looked somewhat reassured and agreed to try again.

"Maybe we go," Tsutomu said to me. "They have to wait for her to get relaxed. It takes a long time. Anyway, we think it's better not too many people watching."

So we started out again for my sister's house. "What was wrong with that girl?" I asked.

"Because she was too much surprised," Tsutomu answered, "so she became afraid."

"No, I mean, what was the reason she needed help? Was she sick or something? Or do you know?"

He did, but he had no idea how to say it in English. I supposed I did not need to know. It was Takahashi's demonstration with the young man that had looked so curious. "Do you think Takahashi San made any red marks on me that time in San Francisco?"

"We can't know because you wore your clothes. Anyway, that time he didn't get his sword to you."

"What do you think the sword does? He doesn't really cut anybody."

"He cuts, I think. Something cuts in some way. I am sure he is not going to use sword if he doesn't need to use it."

Tsutomu was right. The sword had indeed done something, and the effect had been very apparent. "But he didn't cut through the skin," I said. "There was blood, but it wasn't running out."

"Not the skin. It's the same that we talked about before.

72

Takahashi San is understanding electricity body. What is the word we said about that electricity?"

"Current?"

"We can call it soft body because it is consisting of current only. Motion of electricity. It's the same to Rolling Thunder, just like you know. It's the same, only different technique. Except for modern technology, every healer is similar, don't you think? They are all making contact to soft body."

● ● ●

Soft body. Tsutomu was right. "They are all making contact to soft body." Swamis and yogis call it subtle body. In the West we hear etheric body or energy body. Rolling Thunder just called it the body, because to him a being is a spirit whose instrument is an energy structure. Rolling Thunder seemed to see it as "electricity," also. He spoke about the positive and negative polarity of the body—and when he worked with this polarity, he did not touch the skin-encapsulated part of the body that is most easily visible. He once explained a technique in his healing regimen in terms of the controlled use of an electric charge. "All the things that are true about electricity are at work everywhere," he said. "We could say we are working with a kind of electricity energy."

Whether using reflexology, acupuncture, crystals, medicine fans, or laying on of hands—to mention only a few— healers and medicine people of perhaps all periods and places presume to work with current and polarity in a body that is essentially energy—not meat and bones exclusively. The meat-and-bones approach is not without its apparent results, but the holistic view suggests many more subtle alternative approaches that work in cases where physically intrusive tactics are unnecessarily employed.

But what about the samurai? I knew only a little about the samurai of Japan's fascinating cultural history—not enough to know where, or whether, Takahashi fit in. Samurai means "those who serve," but the services of the samurai belong to history. The samurai of today have their training, but it is training for playing the samurai role. The samurai of today (with Takahashi, who walked the city streets in full regalia,

73

being the only exception I ever knew) are to be found in the theater. Takahashi was learned in the history and philosophy of the samurai, however, according to his Japanese followers, and I decided that his assumed exterior identity served some purpose of which at least he was aware.

The capacity for sensing for which Aki had been trained may have been part of the martial arts skill of the samurai of the past. The old farmer and the mudang had sensed me— not only my feelings but also something of my background. Takahashi had sensed my physical discomfort as I sat quietly on the floor while he and Tsutomu talked. Tsutomu had suggested that in the time of the samurai such capacity was not uncommon but that "in modern time most of people just forget about it."

Swami Rama not only put his finger, gently, through hard objects, but he also sensed incoming phone calls and dashed for the receiver, only to produce a busy signal on the other end. "What's the matter?" he would say. "Someone is calling and the telephone is not functioning." This happened frequently when I was his assistant, and I found it necessary to explain to him that the connection is not complete until the ringing sound is heard.

Rolling Thunder had "heard" my howl and had checked to see whether I was trying to reach him. In the years that I had spent with him, he had phoned me only once before—when I had left a message requesting that he contact me. Now he had stopped his car at a pay phone, assuming that I was calling. Had it occurred to me at the time, I might have asked, "What made you think I was trying to reach you?" It is not likely that I would have questioned him, however, and even less likely that he would have offered a descriptive explanation. It is probably no more a wonder that he "heard" me over all those miles than that he had "smelled" those strangers in the shed several yards away. Hearing and smelling, in any case, are nothing other than signals received in the sensorium—the "perceiver" in the brain.

The mudang sensed our arrival. Perhaps, as Koh suggested, she had arranged it somehow, but at any rate, she felt our approach. And Aki claimed he should have sensed the approach of the thieves in the park. Though it may be disappointing to those romantically intrigued with the "supernatural" and the "unexplainable," these phenomena (they do exist) must be explained in terms of the nature of energy. There is no so-called "supernatural."

People like Takahashi are magicians. Magic is not supernatural. Neither is it sleight of hand. Magic is the skillfully controlled manipulation of energy to manifest results in the physical realm. The word is akin to words like "magistrate" and "magnificent." Magic is the result on the physical level of conscious control from a higher level. That is simply its true meaning. The "magicians" we have become accustomed to are people pretending to be magicians. Through trickery, they can make it appear as though they are using magic. But they are not really magicians, and we know it. As with the genuine magician, the methods generally do not meet the eye and the puzzle can be entertaining. Still, the true sense of the word should not be spoiled—for real magicians are everywhere, and many of them are healers. They work with cause and effect in a natural way. There is no "supernatural."

In the materialistic mind-set of modern times, there are those who prefer to insist on the nonexistence of whatever they are unable to see—but it is difficult to argue a case on the basis of an absence of evidence. Indeed, Rolling Thunder and Takahashi can see what they are doing. They can see the subtle bodies of their subjects as clearly as anyone has ever seen anyone. From the subtle body point of view, the gross body is its harder (more readily visible), outer shell that cannot be manipulated but by energy—that is, by the subtle body. When Rolling Thunder and Takahashi perform their medicine, it is for them a matter of a subtle body working on a subtle body. This is, of course, always the case, even in surgery; but with a wider, more complete perspective, more options come to view. The genuine medicine people always see the total view.

"If a modern M.D. sees a sick man, he sees the sickness

and not the man," Rolling Thunder once said to me. "So if the doctor doesn't understand what's going on, what the problem really is, and if he then gives some chemicals so the man won't feel anything, or if he finds some troubled part of the body and cuts it off and throws it in the trash, it's probably all unnecessary, and it certainly isn't healing."

So the subtle approach is to work with cause and effect from the cause side rather than the effect side. The present prevalence of the gross approach may yield yet again in modern times to more subtle and less intrusive healing strategies as new research begins to shed light on the seminal relationship of energy to matter. In any case, traditional healers and medicine people of all ages have maintained many effective healing methods which manifest physical results without emphasis on gross physical procedures. One would have to be arrogant and condescending to an extreme to suppose that any culture on Earth could have been so inane as to perpetuate some diligently practiced and perfected procedure on countless cases, century after century, and never notice that it never worked. It worked.

◐   ◐   ◐

Rolling Thunder often repeated, "We do so many unnatural things, we don't know what's natural anymore." One day he and I were sitting on the ground out in the desert. He was describing a young Indian apprentice from another tribe and making designs in the sand with a stick. Suddenly he said, "You people don't even know what a human being is!" I did not see the connection between the subject at hand and that sudden exclamation, but I had learned to understand what he meant by "you people." It was not a judgmental finger-pointing to be taken personally, but a sort of generalized identification to be applied wherever it fit. "You can look right at someone's empty body and think that you're lookin' at the person when they're not even there. Time and time again, you people speed to the scene of an accident, pick up an empty body and take it down the highway at eighty miles an hour, leaving the person miles behind, not knowing what the heck is going on!" He had made his point apparently, and he stopped. It was an important point—a life-or-death issue, perhaps. I did not know what had brought this on, but it was a matter that had suddenly occurred to him I ought to consider.

As an example, he then described to me an episode in which he went into the hospital to assist a young lady—a friend of friends—who had been in a head-on collision and was a long time in a coma. "I agreed to go in there," he said, "not knowin' what I was gonna, have to do, not understanding completely what was wrong with her. We went in during visiting hours, and I told one of my people to look up the hall and another to watch down the hall, 'cause I didn't want some nurse or doctor walkin' in on me. But the moment I took a good look at the body, I could see she wasn't even there. I had to find her—go get her—and she was way out in the field where the car'd flipped over the cliff, and she was sittin' on a rock. Her friend who was driving was killed. And this one sittin' on the rock, she didn't even know where she was. But, boy, she was determined to stay there. She was totally disoriented. I had to pull her, nearly force her back. Only time we can do that is when we know their own will isn't working—otherwise we always leave it up to their own choice.

"Well, in the early days, most everyone could tell when a person wasn't in their body. That was just natural to see that. That's been lost now, mostly. Only thing I can say is, until you learn to understand these things, you should never, never move an unconscious body. Unconscious means the person is not in there. So treat the body on the scene and never, never move it. Not until you learn how. People can't find their own way back to their body—not when they've been pulled loose that way by some accident or something. Time and time again, traumatized people get abandoned that way. Time and time again, people die in a coma because of that. You oughta put the cases together—figure it out for yourselves."

Some time later, I happened to be talking with the person who had been watching down the hall. Somehow, the subject had come up, and when he learned that I knew about that

*particular event, he shared his own impression. He told me
he had been posted just inside the room to watch out
through the doorway to his left, but as soon as he realized
Rolling Thunder was sound asleep and snoring in the chair,
he himself came in and sat down, seeing no purpose in his
being a lookout. "But Rolling Thunder must have done
something," he said. "Maybe he does it in his sleep. Because
when he woke up, she woke up. They opened their eyes at
the same time. Rolling Thunder looked at her and she just
looked at the ceiling."*

*Occasionally I shared with others who knew Rolling Thun-
der this episode that he had shared with me. Once, when I
had told the story to a group of friends in California, one of
them spoke up in a surprised tone of voice. "I never heard it
that way before. I never knew it. I knew her real well, but I
never heard about that. But now it all makes sense. Let me
tell you what she told me—because I talked to her, right
there in the hospital, before she got out. She remembered
the whole thing like a vivid dream—but only up to the part
where Rolling Thunder came. She just said something pulled
her away. She felt the impact of the crash and then she
passed out, and she dreamed she was floating in the field—
she and her friend. They saw the car upside down and
smashed, but they couldn't connect any meaning to it. They
just floated through the field. It's like people would walk on
the moon, she told me. But then her friend went higher and
higher and she couldn't get up that high. So she called, 'Wait
for me,' but her friend kept going up. And her friend said, 'I
can't wait. You stay, I'm leaving.' So she sat down on a rock,
because she couldn't follow, and she shouted out she would
wait right there. The friend was almost out of sight and she
called down, 'Don't wait for me. When I come back I will have
changed my clothes, and you won't even recognize me.' She
waited for a long, long time. She couldn't figure out anything. The only thing in the world she knew was her friend
and that rock she was sitting on. After a long time—she
didn't know how long—something pulled her off that rock.
Something pulled her through space until she woke up from
her dream."*

Our little group sat silently for a long while, thinking about what all this meant. "It's true," someone remarked, "there's so much we've got to regain. So much we've lost that we've got to get back. It's not even a thing of trying to be extraordinary or far out. There's just certain things we have to know for the sake of our everyday lives—things we've just got to remember before the whole human scene falls apart."

Rolling Thunder, whose healing methodology requires that he see not only physical bodies but also etheric bodies, had induced me to consider the importance of the capacity to see the astral body—to see beyond the structure he referred to as the body and to see what he called the person. But one must see a person with one's own person—not with one's carcass!

In his healing practice Rolling Thunder administered to the subtle part of the body as well as the dense part—etheric body to etheric body. The etheric body belongs to the physical structure, to the carcass, and with practice it can be seen —with what we might call waking vision. It is the energy matrix that interpenetrates and extends slightly beyond the denser part. As the girl sat on the rock in the field and waited, knowing nothing but her friend, it was her corporeal form— the physical/etheric or the matter/energy structure—that lay on the bed in a comatose state. The "person" was not there. What Rolling Thunder calls the person is the noncorporeal, conscious, living self that may or may not be there with the physical/etheric part. When he found the girl sitting on the rock in the field, he did not see her with his physical eyes— they were closed and far behind in the hospital as his body sat snoring in the chair. It was an astral body finding an astral body.

Beyond the view of that from which matter manifests lies the view of that from which energy emanates. I can tell you what I see, but I cannot tell you what you cannot see. We are not in a position to tell the mystic, the magician, or the medicine person what is not there and cannot, therefore, be seen. But we are in a position—when someone tells us what is there that we ought to see—to make some effort to look!

79

SCENE FIVE

Ask and You
Shall Be Pushed

Riding the roads of India in a minibus can be a bumpy business, and the road south was long and tiring. We were on our way to visit Rajalakshmi, a professor and yogini whom we had met some weeks before in Kanpur. I was traveling as an independent writer with a psychophysiological research team from The Menninger Foundation, and I was looking forward to our arrival—to seeing Rajalakshmi again and, especially, to getting out of the minibus.

Mahayogini Rajalakshmi was living in the town of Tirupati in the province of Andhra Pradesh in southern India. This small city, not far northeast of Madras, is the home of the famous god Sri Venkateshwara—the wealthiest deity in all of India and one of the richest in the world. He and his female counterpart reside in the temple at the top of the mountain that overlooks the city. People come by the thousands—year around, from all over India to make their offerings. Rich and poor alike give significant portions of their assets, or even shear and sell their hair at the stalls along the approach to the temple and journey home with bald heads (for there is a good chance that this great god might see fit to return their offerings tenfold); and so this temple acquires riches, second only, it is told, to St. Peter's in Rome. Lahks and lahks of rupees, as the townspeople put it, are thus made available to this community, and Tirupati can boast some of the finest educational and medical facilities in all of India.

Mahayogini Rajalakshmi was a professor of biochemistry at Sri Padmavathi, Tirupati's famous university for women. In addition, she operated at her home a free clinic as well as an institute for the instruction of Jnana yoga. Rajalakshmi was both a professor and a yogi, and she had college students, yoga students, patients, and disciples. Her name and title suited her: a mahayogini is a highly advanced, or "great," female yogi adept; the word *raja* implies royalty; and Lakshmi, her namesake, is Hinduism's goddess of prosperity. She was the descendant of one of India's wealthy maharajas and the daughter of a prince—though as a yogi, she had detached herself from personal involvement with the wealth that she possessed.

The town of Tirupati was on our travel route, and a visit to Mahayogini Rajalakshmi was part of our agenda. There were nine of us crowded into our rented minibus, including our driver Chotti, as we traveled thousands of miles around India. In addition to all of us, there were dozens of suitcases and trunks which contained the physiological monitoring and recording equipment, the cameras and apparatus for the film crew, and our personal luggage. My parents, Elmer and Alyce Green, and my sister Judy were the research team; Elda Hartley of Hartley productions and her two assistants, Harvey Bellin and Tom Kieffer, were the film crew; and Dolly Gattozzi and I were writers. The three-month project was to study the voluntary control of psychophysiological states and states of consciousness of yogi adepts, to obtain scientific data, and to produce a documentary film.

When we had first met Rajalakshmi at the All India Yoga Conference, which was sponsored by Swami Rama's institute in Kanpur, she had not looked like a yogi to me: She differed not only from the stereotypical image we Westerners have been given but also from every other yogi at the conference (and also, I was to discover, from every other yogin or yogini I ever saw in India). She wore colorful saris and costly jewels. She was young and exuberant and had the striking beauty and bearing of one of India's romantic film stars.

I supposed that Manoharlal Dudeja considered himself a disciple of hers, though he never said so directly. Manoharlal Dudeja was a successful businessman in the industrial city of Kanpur, and he was our first host in India while we attended the All India Yoga Conference. His large, comfortable Kanpur home accommodated our group nicely, and during the hours we spent with him in his sitting room, he spoke often of Rajalakshmi.

Rajalakshmi had been somewhat of a legend in her own hometown during her childhood, we were told. As a child, she had begun to meditate and had experienced many occurrences of transcending gravity. At times she would levitate, and at times she would turn upside down and balance on her head. At one period she turned upside down so often that it wore away the hair on the top of her head. And then, she was so often and so long in levitation that people came from near and far to see her. These things had occurred spontaneously, Manoharlal explained, and were not entirely in her control. It created a problem for her wealthy family, and they had to hire guards because of the crowds. Now, however, she had become an earthly and practical person. She was a scholar and a teacher, and there were many with whom she worked who knew nothing of her past.

It would be good to have a chance to spend some time with her at her own place, but it seemed to take an eternity to get to Tirupati. Since Kanpur, we had seen a variety of people and places, and we had nearly become accustomed —though not entirely adjusted—to long hours on such bumpy and dusty roads. It was late afternoon when at last we arrived in Tirupati and stopped to ask directions. Chotti located the address with little difficulty, and both Judy and I went up to knock on Rajalakshmi's door while the others waited in the minibus.

Her name and address were on the front of the house.

There was another door at the left with a carved wooden sign that said POLIO CLINIC. That door opened. By her flashing eyes, sparkling smile, and outward manner, it was easy to know that she was happy to see us. She rushed out, leaving the door standing open, offered warm salutations to Judy and me, and hastened down the walk toward the minibus, loudly greeting the others as she approached. But she turned abruptly and looked back at the open door, and I wondered whether I should close it for her. Then I noticed a little face peeking around the doorframe. She shouted loudly, and a small boy stepped out. He appeared to be struggling between his curiosity and his shyness. She shouted again and her manner surprised me. I had been aware of her energetic straightforwardness, but now she was commanding this little fellow in English, insisting that he get into the minibus and greet the visitors, and she seemed somewhat demanding. He started down the walk and she clapped her hands, inducing him to run and to jump into the bus. When everyone had said hello to him, he started to climb backward through the high door of the vehicle, putting a hand up to brace himself and stretching one leg to reach the ground. Again she clapped her hands together, insisting that he turn around and jump. He did it well, landing grace-fully on both feet, and he looked pleased with himself as he ran back up the walk.

Rajalakshmi rode with us to the guesthouse of Sri Venka-teshwara University, where we were to be accommodated during our stay. We learned on the way that the little boy was one of her patients in her polio clinic. He had not appeared to be even slightly afflicted, I thought. But perhaps that could explain why she had been so insistent. We also learned that many of the scholars and physicians connected with the medical college of this university, as well as a number of government officials—and the chief of police of this city—were students of Rajalakshmi.

It occurred to Harvey that she might be able to help him. Over the past several days he had been suffering from a severe cold and had decided perhaps he had some serious

83

sinus ailment or allergy. After we were settled in at the guest-house and Rajalakshmi was about to leave us, he brought the matter up with her.

"You come in the morning!" she said without hesitation. "We shall clear it up in the morning."

Harvey wondered about the schedule for the morning and whether he could make himself available to take advantage of her help. Perhaps Chotti could drive him. "What are the plans for tomorrow?" he inquired of the group.

"No, no! You will come in the morning. You will be back before breakfast. So you have only to reach my house by four a.m."

Harvey was not exactly an easy riser, even at normal waking hours. "Maybe we should wait," he said. "It's probably just all the dust from the roads, and it'll clear up in a day or so. Or maybe you could suggest something I could take."

"Come on, Harvey," someone said. "Don't try to get out of it. You know you've been miserable."

Rajalakshmi laughed. "No, no, he will definitely come. You will see."

She was right. It was his discomfort and his need for help and it was also that insistent manner of hers that made it happen. It was still only dawn when he returned, and we had not yet gathered for breakfast. He looked so sleepy when he came to my room that at first I was afraid he had missed his appointment.

"I'm not sleepy," he said. "I'm in shock. I can't believe what happened. I had water running in one nostril and out the other, and down my throat and up again, and strings and stuff going in my nose and out my mouth—I can't believe the things I did! You remember all that funny stuff some of the yogis demonstrated at the conference? I did all that myself. And I'm the last person in the world who'd try any of that stuff. Maybe I was half spaced out when I got there or something. Before I knew what was going on, I was doing it." He thought for a moment, shaking his head. "Actually, she made me do it. She simply made me. I can't say she forced me exactly, but there was no way I could have gotten out of it. It's like if someone steps up to you and suddenly shouts, 'Jump!' you just jump."

That made me think for a moment about that little boy. "Well, it seems to have worked," I said. "In any case, you've got to admit, you asked her."

"Yeah, and I guess it did do the trick," he acknowledged. "But what I wonder is—how the hell did I know how to even do that stuff?"

Rajalakshmi arrived at the guesthouse wearing a beautiful sari and driving a bright red convertible. It made an interesting impression. I had never seen such a vehicle in India. Many of the well-to-do rode about in their standard-looking domestic sedans, driven by their hired drivers; but she was driving this sporty little car herself, and she was a woman— and a yogi at that. The red convertible, we learned, belonged to the chief of police, who made it available for her occasional errands. We also learned that this local lawman was another of the yogini's disciples and that we would be meeting him that evening. Our entire group had been invited to his home.

When dinner was served, there were about a dozen of us, including our group and his family—all seated around one long table in his living room. It was a beautiful Indian meal followed by fragrant tea and sweetmeats. A basin and towel were brought around so that we could rinse our hands at the table. We sat for a long while and talked. Some of us questioned our host about his work. We wondered about the difference between our country and India in matters of crime and law enforcement. We knew of various incidents of widespread unrest over issues of religious and political control; but it was hard to imagine acts of interpersonal violence—at least among the people of these quiet villages and holy cities.

"We have no crimes of violence or malice in this city," the police chief told us, "and few crimes of passion. The crimes that we see might be called crimes of the stomach."

He spoke for a moment about his town and his people, and then about their culture and customs. Soon he was tell-

85

ing us about Rajalakshmi, praising her abilities and her many contributions to others, as she sat and listened. For all he knew, he was our only way of learning these things about her, and he wanted us to have an appreciation of her beyond what she would tell of herself. We heard about some of the people he knew whom she had helped, and then he decided to tell about himself. Mahayogini had cured him completely of the diabetes he had had nearly all his life. He described in detail his diagnosis and prescribed medication, his regimen of self-testing and administering of insulin. He told of how she had worked with him for years with her steady and disciplined methods of yoga, diet, breathing, and self-regulation. He was at last completely free of his diabetes and his need for insulin.

His eyes became wet as he expressed his reverence and appreciation for her. His sharing had been for his own benefit as well as ours, it seemed. This may have been his only opportunity to articulate his gratitude for Rajalakshmi in a way that she could hear it.

Rajalakshmi spent the next day working with the research and film crews and the biomedical lab. She had not been a subject herself but had arranged for two of her disciples to be "wired up" as she demonstrated the effects of *shaktipat*, or "power touch": the transference of energy, or the energizing of chakras. With one of her students in particular there was a demonstrable effect; as she executed the shaktipat, his heart rate decreased. As he sat on the floor in front of her and she sat lotus-posture behind him, she held the palm of her hand slightly above the top of his head; and her eyelids fluttered, showing only the clear, shiny whites of her eyes on her calm face. It made an impressive image for the film.

One evening at sunset, I sat on the buggy seat of a three-wheeled bicycle rickshaw and rode through the streets of Tirupati to call on Rajalakshmi. I was alone. Judy was in bed, and all the others had left for Madras. I had written the address for the rickshaw walla, but only her name had been enough. Apparently, everyone in this town knew the yogini. The rickshaw, I thought, was the most exciting way to sight-see in this country. One could sit in relative comfort and let the driver do the stopping, starting, and dodging. Walking was more distracting: It took more concentration and often attracted too much attention. The automobile was too insu-lating. From this seat, I could hear and feel the energetic bustle of the streets, and I could even reach out and touch the side of a sacred cow. I was almost unnoticed as I rode, and yet right in the midst of the washing, cooking, shopping, playing—the vivid hubbub of daily life. I was pleased, in a way, to have been left behind and thus to have the opportu-nity to explore on my own.

Judy had become weak a few days earlier and had lost her appetite; and when jaundice began to show in her eyes, hep-atitis was suspected. Among Rajalakshmi's students were a number of medical doctors, and she arranged for Judy to be tested. Our suspicions were confirmed. Since my experience with hepatitis in Korea made me a sympathetic "expert," I was left behind to care for her while the others went on to Madras to continue their research agenda. Her case was not serious, but she needed to spend her days and nights totally at rest. She could not eat more than a little juice or soup, and so I went alone to have dinner at Rajalakshmi's. I regret-ted missing Madras, but I was fortunate indeed to have this extra time with Rajalakshmi.

The rickshaw walla parked his bicycle in front of the house and settled back on the seat to wait. I stood at the door and knocked, but there was no response. The house was dark and it appeared that Rajalakshmi was out, but she was ex-pecting me and I was sure she would return. After a long while, I knocked again, but there was still no response. I decided I should wait for at least another hour, and I was glad that my rickshaw driver had not left me. Eventually, a light came on and she appeared at the door. "I had been in meditation," she said, casually. That was to be considered explanation enough.

She must have prepared our supper in advance before she began her meditation, for it was ready when I arrived. There might have been someone helping in the kitchen, but if so, that person either left or remained out of sight. In any case, I waited at the table for only a moment. She carried our food from the kitchen on a large tray. It was one of the spiciest meals I had ever experienced. Fortunately, I had become well accustomed to extremely hot food through years of living with Mexicans and Koreans and other spice-loving peoples, or I should not have enjoyed this supper at all.

This was also the first meal I ever handled in a totally customary and proper Indian manner. My achievement was owing to this teacher's energetic and assertive coaching style. Through the simple experience of being taught by this yogini how to eat, I could grasp how she worked with her own yoga practice, with her yoga students, college students, and patients, and how, in fact, she had managed the nearly impossible with our friend Harvey. There were no forks or spoons such as our other hosts had provided, and I was tearing off little pieces of chapati with which to grasp my food and lift it to my mouth. This I had tried before, and I was sure I was doing it fairly well, but Rajalakshmi grinned each time I did it. And the rice was a problem—especially since it followed when the chapatis had been eaten and since it was to be mixed with the soupy vegetable dishes or with the creamy yogurt. I was somewhat successful at picking up little pinches of plain, dry rice between my thumb and fingers, but now she laughed out loud.

"Why do you hesitate?" she asked.

"Hesitate? How do you mean?"

"No, no. Just see. You are afraid of your food, isn't it?"

"I don't know. I don't think so."

Soon, with her insistent coaching, I was immersing my hand in mounds of gooey rice and yogurt, squeezing it in my fist so that it oozed out between my fingers, and holding up large handfuls so that the juice ran down my arm and dripped off my elbow. Especially through such overdoing, I could feel myself pushing against my own reluctance.

"It's only food," she said. "Precious food! It cannot hurt

you, only help you. Don't let it get the best of you!" For only a moment I felt awkward, but I could sense that to her this training was both purposeful and fun, and I began to enjoy it. "You see?" she said, "You did have hesitation. Crippling hesitation. And now you have solved it. Such a simple thing, isn't it? And just see how we put up obstacles before each and every step. Even the smallest wish and purpose fights against this holding back!"

I had indeed just experienced a mild version of overcoming. It was that same familiar feeling that had accompanied my first swimming, diving, public speaking, horseback riding—everything I had wished to try. Again she laughed. "Why do you go on as if with some plaything? You can eat now, the problem is solved."

After supper, we began to look at pictures. Her "scrapbook" was a large envelope that contained a stack of photos, notes, clippings, and printed pictures. Among the snapshots of Rajalakshmi were several photographs taken by a newspaper journalist, showing her sitting in lotus-posture and levitating about a foot off the floor. On one of these in particular, it looked as though some external force—almost like a great wind, or perhaps a vacuum—were acting upon her and lifting her into the air. Her hair and her clothing appeared to be blowing in several directions, while her expression and her posture appeared still and calm.

I wondered, looking at these pictures, whether this had been a demonstration for some researcher or reporter. Someone had told Harvey while we were visiting the women's university that she had once demonstrated levitation for a group of students and faculty. I wondered if perhaps it had been a spontaneous demonstration. Harvey was always asking questions, and I had more than once appreciated his assertiveness. I wanted to question her now, but it felt inappropriate at the moment—especially to ask her directly. When Manoharlal Dudeja had told us about her childhood levitations, he had said that it was a totally spontaneous development and that he believed it was no longer occurring.

"It does not happen nowadays," she said, as though feeling my thoughts. "Well, not spontaneously as before. And it was never an objective of mine—not something I was seeking. It was like an automatic sort of thing, and it gave me problems at times. In college I had to stay alone because I had several times alarmed my roommates. This is a surprising thing, you see, when it is so unusual for them and unexpected. My teachers and my superiors have understood me, fortunately. Now they have become my students and they pursue practices with me—not this levitation thing—useful yoga practices."

"Didn't it happen in your childhood?" I asked, at last allowing myself some gentle inquiry. "I heard it began when you were quite young. If it was spontaneous, what was the cause of it?"

For a moment she studied the photograph, and then she turned it face down on the table as though it were obstructive to her recollection. We sat quietly as she reflected. "Just first we should take time for the evening puja. Then we shall talk as we like."

The centerpiece of the puja table looked like a rather makeshift model of a Hindu temple. Inside were the figures of deities sitting or standing along the walls. It could have been an actual temple like many I had seen in this country, depicted here in miniature. There were many little colored lights inside and out, and candles and sticks of incense were lit and placed about on the puja table, making the whole scene alive and enchanting.

The yogini rang a little bell and waved some incense and began to chant. "Ah," she said, turning to me as though something had just occurred to her, "you have not yet heard me play the veena, isn't it? Did you know I have actually learned to play the veena?"

She needed no reply from me. It was time for the veena. I had not noticed it sitting in the corner until she unwrapped it. She placed herself upon a cushion and her instrument against her lap, and she began to pluck the strings. The steady drone of the subdominant sympathetic vibrations filled the room, and she turned her head from side to side as her sliding fingers rendered the mythic melody.

Again she interrupted herself. "You have also not yet seen me dance, isn't it? Although you have, of course, seen me in these photos." I had indeed noticed the small, framed pictures on the wall—photographs that had captured a dancer in dramatic gestures—but I had not known that the dancer was she. Soon she was moving about the room, turning, whirling, bobbing, and miming. But it lasted only a moment, and she was back to her veena.

Several times she danced and played in sequence, and I thought perhaps she was wishing she could perform the music and the dance at the same time. There was no way I could help with this—no way I could participate in her ritual performance—but I tried not to wish that I could, lest I find myself being coached again. Yet, I did not feel uncomfortable watching. Rajalakshmi appeared natural and confident in all that she did, and she carried on her unusual ritual with such determined exuberance that it felt not only appropriate but also important. This was, in any case, all part of her regular puja, I supposed, as she paused, now and again, before her altar to chant and wave incense. This was the way it was done, no doubt, whether anyone else were here or not.

"Actually, I was not a child, you know," she said, returning to the pictures on the table and to our conversation, "not a small child, but a schoolgirl. As a young girl when this happened, I was amazed, I can say, but I was not frightened. Yet it startled my parents. To them it appeared an emergency, something dangerous happening to their daughter, so they were quite upset enough to seek help."

"They were there when it first happened?"

"Not the first time—the third or fourth time, perhaps. You see, I went up, straight up from my bed, which was against the wall. We have these high windows with inside shutters as you have seen, isn't it? And I hit the shutter. Normally I could not reach the shutter, and it made such a loud sound in the night, my parents came rushing in. Seeing me suspended in the air in that manner, they were startled, and my father shouted at me. Perhaps that in itself brought me down, and I became fully conscious."

"So you were asleep when it happened?"

"No, no, I was in meditation, and even though I was not fully conscious of my body, I knew what had happened and why. But I could explain nothing to my parents."

"But you knew why?"

"You see, when I was highest in my class, in this one particular session, I received a gift from my teacher. It is like an award for achievement—it was a practice in our schools to offer such gifts. This time my teacher chose for me a wonderful book, *The Gospel of Sri Ramakrishna.* Do you know this work? I think so. It is a famous thing. But in my family, you see, these things were not there. The emphasis was more on business and practical things. Not that they were opposed to religion, but we did not attend to these things deeply, you see. So I would read this book, and it was so, so inspirational for me, it opened me to something. I used to meditate on this, though I had not been doing meditation. I would read some pages and become so moved, and I would meditate on this emotion. I read it in the evenings instead of my homework. I had not much worry for my homework, as I was excelling in my classwork, and I read this book instead when my parents thought I was doing homework. So this thing did it—it put me into levitation. This book was the cause of it in the beginning."

"Manoharlal told us that you were in levitation so much that it became known, and eventually many people came to witness it."

"Manoharlal told you? You see, this thing does not happen in your country. Not so that it can be known to the people. If someone is doing this, it should be secretly, because it would not be accepted and it would not be understood. If some child should do this unknowingly, it would be utterly and totally denied in your country. Here such things are accepted, generally—and they were not uncommon in the old days. But such a thing as levitation is never attributed to an individual as a personal capacity or success. It would be a confusion and a danger in your society if someone should levitate and be witnessed, because the people would take it to be someone's personal achievement—a sign of some person's loftiness. You see, there everyone is striving for personal gains—either for material commodities or for other admirable assets.

"In my country such a thing is taken to be a manifestation of a higher reality, at least when it is properly understood. One cannot pursue these manifestations because higher reality is manifest when personal aspirations are put aside. I was a young girl, you see, innocent and without ambition. Something in me was profoundly moved, and an opening occurred. Had I wanted it, it would never have happened. Many people came in those days. Twice a week they filed in and out. But it was not to see me as an amazing girl. It was not for fascination that they came. Not even for confirmation or encouragement—not those, in any case, who came in proper attitude. For centuries in my country it has been a practice of religious pilgrims to see such a situation. They simply seek to be in that presence. They only want a moment of contact with one who is seen to be in the presence of some divine universal principle. It is that principle they wish to meet, and not the person."

"How did they know about you? Manoharlal said they came from many far places."

"It started in my village, and then it spread. It started because my parents sought help in my village. They went to the old man who was considered the leading sage in our village. He had many followers, and though my parents were not among them, they knew about this old man. So they told about me, what had happened. By this time, they also knew about the book, and they had told me to put the book away and leave it. The old man said they had come to the wrong person. 'When she is having her living guru, why do you not go to her guru?' he said. 'And then he will come to your daughter.' So they went by train to find my guru according to the old man's instructions. He knew, you see, because they know these things. And my guru was aware already, and he scolded my parents, saying it was by their own ignorance that they were so worried while their daughter was not. He assured them he would come, but only after several weeks' time. And they were told in the meantime to let me be and let me read my book. They were told that nothing would harm me, unless it be their own fears.

"So then it went on for a time. I went on reading my book and remaining long hours in meditation and long hours in levitation. I did not go to school, and I stopped taking meals, taking only warm milk from time to time. So the villagers learned of this and they came. Others began to arrive from here and there. My father would not let them see me, and at last there were crowds of people—men, women, children—sleeping and washing and preparing meals on our property. My father was wealthy and had huge lands, and hundreds of people were camping. So, by my father's influence, many policemen were stationed. But they could not make the people leave. They convinced my parents that the crowds would become disorderly. The safest way would be to satisfy the people. If my parents would agree to a controlled schedule, the people would become totally cooperative. The policemen have had experience in these matters. So the days of the week and the hours were set, and the people could come in, a few at a time, in one door and out the other. There were ropes put between so they could not touch me.

"During those many weeks, I was mostly unaware of all this. Then one day my guru arrived, and he said it is time that I came down. 'You were born into this world and here you belong,' he said. 'You have your work to do, or you would not have come. And you are lost in your bliss. Look at you! You are weak and helpless! Do you want to be useless in this lifetime? Is this why you have come to this world? To go on and on with this?' "

Rajalakshmi sat quietly for a while. I could sense that she was recalling the words and the presence of her guru. She picked up the photograph that lay face down on the table, glanced at it, and turned it face down again. "Now I will show you the boy. You have met this boy."

She filed through the stack of photographs until she came to the one she wanted, and she handed it to me. I recognized him only because I knew who he had to be. I had met only one small boy here. This had to be the little fellow who had come running and skipping down the walk and had jumped into our minibus on the day that we arrived. But here he was standing on spindly little legs, held up by two adults who were grasping an arm on either side. These legs were so twisted and deformed that there was no way the boy could walk or run or even stand on his own. Yet I had seen him do it.

"How he has changed, isn't it? And not much more than one year's time, he has done it!"

I tried to picture the little boy jumping in and out of the minibus as I studied the deformed legs in the photograph. They were entirely different legs. How could such a total change occur in such a brief amount of time, I wondered.

"Through yoga such things can happen, you see? Yoga exercises. Physical exercises are there, so many kinds of physical exercises. And breathing exercises are essential. Without the proper breathing development, you see, the changes do not come. Breathing controls everything. People do not understand the relevance of this breathing practice. So when we attend to the diet, posture, exercise, sleep, and all healthy habits, we must not forget to attend to the breathing. Consciously it must be developed in order that all these things may take their proper benefit. Without attentive practice, it will not develop correctly."

"I can see the relevance of all these things—and of the breathing exercises—to general good health," I said. "For strength and stamina and even prevention of disease and depression I can understand how it would be effective. But how can it make a change like this? I mean, this boy's legs have been completely redeveloped."

"Because that is the goal, you see? Whatever is the goal, we must fix our minds upon that clearly. We can see it clearly, what is to be developed. This is the same thing—visualization—that the Greens have been talking in all this research. The legs are completely redeveloped, but this is quite naturally done by the body. The body has developed the legs in everyone's case, isn't it? Countless, countless cells are continuously produced and reproduced, and bones and tissues are developed according to the picture which is supplied by the mind. So here the visualization comes. But we must supply also the means for the body. Through all these practices and exercises, the proper chemistry and all the subtle energies will be there. Now it becomes an act of the body itself, isn't it?"

"Right," I responded. "So, through these exercises, the body is supplying the necessary means to and for itself."

"But at the same time, the body will resist, you see? This is the point. It is so, so much work. The body does not resist the change—the change comes—but the body resists the effort. This is the reason, you may know, I pushed him. I pushed and pushed and pushed, and there was no escape for him. Otherwise he will not make such tremendous effort, daily, daily, for so many months, which no one will do—especially child."

"It makes me think of Harvey."

"Harvey? Harvey is a nice man. He is much better now with his condition. He came to see me, you know."

"I know, he talked to me that morning. I was thinking about that pushing because Harvey said he found himself doing things he'd never do—and could hardly believe he did."

"Ah, but you see, he did it. It was his desire and he asked me. He said, 'Can you help me?' So I pushed him because he asked me. Without such request I would never prevail upon anyone. The arrangement is made according to the request. Otherwise, it becomes an interference, and it is a useless thing—a mischievous thing. You may be right to think Harvey would not have done these things without me. But Harvey treated himself, isn't it? He treated himself by his own request. So it is with the boy. He treated himself. It must be by his own effort. How else can it be? And the boy's case was not a simple matter like it was with Harvey. You should have seen his effort! Trying, trying, falling, and crying while I pushed him so. Yet in the boy's case, fortunately, as he was a growing child, we had a nice chance to influence the development as it came and make changes."

"I can really appreciate the effort that he made even though I can't imagine it. But wasn't a request for help important in the boy's case? Was it because he was a child? Or did his father ask for help?"

"Acha! The father, indeed! We may say the father, but it was not the earthly parent who came to me. It was the father within him. Or let us say it is the father within whom exists the child. This is the true being. This is the one who came to me. He implored me because I could provide the techniques. I knew how it could be done. But together we arranged the details. I pushed only because I myself was pushed. And how beautifully the child cooperated! Because through me, you see, actually he pushed himself. It works in this way with all of us. It is an absolutely wonderful thing!"

I still held the photograph. I looked again at those twisted little legs, and again I recalled him as I had seen him. Then I pictured him as a college student and wondered what his childhood experience might mean to him then. I should like to see that boy again.

"How do you go back?" she asked. "It comes to be late, and you will have to seek some conveyance."

"No, the rickshaw's waiting outside," I answered, and I looked out to confirm it.

"Oh, is it? Well, you have money enough to pay him properly and make it worth his while. Don't you be a stingy, wealthy American, and you just give him plenty. We must pay well, according to our means, especially to those in need. It always helps far more than it harms. But just you wait. I'll pour one more cup of tea before you make your move."

◐   ◐   ◐

Every time I recall how I knocked and waited and knocked again on the door of that dark house while Rajalakshmi was meditating inside, apparently unaware of the time, I get a strong image of her sitting lotus-posture in the dark—about

97

a foot off the floor. I don't know that she was in levitation when I arrived for dinner that night—but it is the image that comes to mind. "It doesn't happen anymore," she had told me. "Not spontaneously." But did she allow herself to rise from time to time?

I think about people I've known—Westerners—who have really worked at it, struggling to bob an inch or two for a brief second, with such determination, according to their own reports, that their very effort seemed to be an obstacle. Rajalakshmi, as a young schoolgirl, read a book and up she went. It was because, as she put it, she was moved. She was, in her own words, "innocent and without ambition," but something in her was "profoundly moved."

This yogini was one of the most joyful and vivacious people I've known. But she had no sense of personal success. Her guru had told her to come down and be useful. And useful she was: she was an important professor in a leading university, she was a guide and teacher to a number of disciples, she ran a yoga institute as well as a clinic, and she was an adept and a healer. "But such things," I can hear her say, "cannot be attributed to me as a personal capacity or success." It seems to me now, as I recall her music and her dance, her sharing of her photographs and some of her life, that in everything she did, she was either moved or pushed. "I pushed and pushed," she said, referring to her work with the little boy, "only because I myself was pushed."

Rolling Thunder explained that a true medicine person can show availability and willingness but can never conduct a healing without an invocation. "We never do anything to work on a person," he said, "unless we're asked." Sometimes, he would say, it is the "spirit" who does the asking. As in the case of the "father" within whom the little boy existed, it seems to be the entitlement of the higher self not simply to ask but to implore—even to insist. Rolling Thunder once told me about a time he attended a conference at a clinic and agreed to work on a few patients to be selected by the medical doctors there. One young man who had not been selected woke him up in the middle of the night to insist that he be brought forward on the following day. It was the young man's "spirit," Rolling Thunder explained to me, who had to make the arrangements because the "man" was too self-conscious and withdrawn.

When Swami Rama was asked to help a young boy who had been diagnosed as having a severe case of asthma, Swami said it was the boy's heart that was the problem. "I called the boy, and he came to me in his astral body," Swami later explained, "and he told me that he had come into this lifetime with a defective heart. When I asked him whether he wanted my help, he said that he did."

There are those who have spoken of the guru-chela (master-disciple) relationship in these same terms. Swami Kaivalyananda, the scholar swami of the Sivananda Ashram in Muni Ki Reti, told me that the guru is "you." The real guru in this view is the higher self, and the external one called guru is one who, qualified by his or her own advanced evolution, functions as the mirror in cooperation with the chela's higher self.

This concept of a higher, knowing self and a lower, un-knowing self is found in the original traditions and mysticism of virtually all cultures and religions; but it is rare in the modern West where science does not look beyond the material world or the mechanical self and religious fundamentalism denies the knowing self and attributes fault and sin even to the soul.

The dynamic will that is the higher self is the very source of mind and matter. All substance in all the physical kingdoms—every single multiplicity of atoms and molecules—is held in form by the power of thought. In every manifest being the creative force is the higher self—the dynamic will the yogini called "the Father." In every living earthly form, the mind is the controlling factor. All creativity, causation, cultivation, and change spring from the source to the surface. Healing happens from the inside out. Healers and helpers can be movers and pushers. They can offer help, hope, sympathy, and support. But they do not allow their own works and ways to pretermit the creative will of their subjects. They work knowingly with the natural process of creative transformation. Every healing, growth, development, and change is generated within and manifests outwards.

●　　　　●　　　　●

One of my sisters, Dr. Patricia Norris, now a therapist at The Menninger Foundation, once came out to visit me in Oakland for a few weeks. At that time, she was a psychologist at the Kansas Reception and Diagnostic Center, where she worked with prisoners. Over many years, with pupils, prisoners, and patients, she had experienced and helped others to experience how the mind and the emotions—how images and expectations—can influence one's condition and one's circumstances and play an important role in the outcome of events.

One day, just as we were walking out to her van in front of my apartment, there was an accident about a block up the street. We did not see it, but I heard it or felt it, at least unconsciously, for something snapped at my attention, and I moved around the van to look up in that direction just in time to see a man go scraping across the pavement on his head, with his arms and legs flying in the air. I could only stand and blink my eyes, but I must have made some sound, because my sister, almost inside the van behind the wheel, stepped out, looked where I was looking, and without a moment's pause, went dashing up the street.

I followed along behind, but with some hesitation, wondering what either she or I could do but call for help. She was way ahead of me, and I saw her kneel down on the pavement and lean over the man whose head lay in a puddle of blood. Was she trying to see if he was conscious or trying to wake him up? A motorcycle lay in the street several yards away, and on the sidewalk was a Volkswagen bug. I ran up and stood beside her. I could see there was no one in the car, and I assumed the driver had gone somewhere to call.

My sister had her hands cupped over the man's ear. She must have been talking into that bloody head, though I could

100

not hear her words, for the man was responding and his tone of voice did not at all match his appearance: "I hear you, I hear you," he was saying. "Keep on talkin'. Right on, sister, you got it, you got it. I don't wanna pass out. Just don't stop talkin' to me." We heard the sirens approaching, and the man went on mumbling, "Just keep it up, my friend, keep on talkin'." A policeman arrived first, and then the ambulance, and when the man was taken away, we started back down the street toward the van.

"What were you doing there?" I asked. "What were you saying to him?"

"I just ran up, knelt down, put my mouth in his ear and my mind in his mind, and helped him focus on what was happening. I told him the accident was over. We always get locked in on the trauma and stay focused on that. It's natural, but it really impedes healing. So I told him, 'You're finished being injured now. You have to remind yourself of that. The accident is over, and you're as injured as you're going to get. The healing has started. You're not being injured anymore, you're already being repaired. The minute we get hurt, the healing process begins. Just cooperate with the healing. Focus on that because that's what's happening. See if you can feel it. Try to feel your body doing its repairing work. Acknowledge the healing, because it will help it a lot.' I just went on like that, and fortunately, he really got into it."

The man was no doubt benefited by someone's being there to help his mind help himself—someone who understood how healing works and who was willing to be involved in this way. In his case, after his injury, he also benefited from the availability of crisis-intervention treatment. Either assistance without the other would have been less effective. But, essentially, he healed himself. Likewise, so did the little boy with the crippled legs heal himself. His knowing self knew enough to seek help on the interpersonal level; but, essentially, he healed himself. It is never any other way. He could not have done it alone—not because he was a child, but because he was a person. People live, work, grow, and heal together—these are mutual endeavors.

"Rugged individualism" may be so coined because it is uneven, turbulent and stormy—a sort of bittersweet combination of self-satisfaction and bitter loneliness. It may have its place, but it is certainly not very "together." It's a popular word, these days, that word together. People say it again and again; "Get it together." Well, we'll have to do it together. You just can't "get it together" alone. One literally cannot pull up on one's own bootstraps, as some have enjoyed imagining, and get much of a lift. My father once told me that in hell everyone has a tablespoon attached to his or her elbow. The hungrier they get, the more antisocial, and it does not occur to them to feed one another. It's hell because they can't get their elbows to their mouths.

It is intriguing to consider that the powerful and universal healing force, ever present within each and every one of us, requires the catalytic force of mutuality, of caring and support. Individual self-sufficiency, it appears, is supported by the principle of interrelatedness and the interconnectedness of all of life. We can all feel, along with our sense of self-sufficiency, our basic need for one another. We can all sense the need in our contemporary culture for direct, interpersonal human support systems.

The new (for us, at any rate) holistic concepts of health and healing are based upon the recognition of and regard for body, mind, and spirit. But the interconnectedness of body, mind, and spirit functions within the interconnectedness of all of life. Responsibility for health and healing does not reside within the individual. It resides within the arrangement and agreement that unites all life.

There is no personal growth, human potential, or ultimate health outside of a social and cultural context of belonging and caring and mutual support—the essential conditions—the only circumstances—in which true healing can happen.

Consider the concept of self-sufficiency—the concept that on the highest level we are always in control of our own destinies. Consider the concept of mutual interdependence—the reality that on the human level there is a constant need for caring, compassion, and concurrence. Consider the concept of a healing principle—a natural, universal force ever at work in every living organism. Consider, also, the knowledge and willingness that is available to others through such persons as Rajalakshmi and through movers and pushers appearing in increasing numbers in our culture in the area of the healing arts. To consider all these concepts in terms of how they work together is extremely heartening. It is, as Rajalakshmi said, "an absolutely wonderful thing!"

SCENE SIX

The Monk
From the Past

Shozo phoned me from San Francisco to say that he and
Mitziko wanted to bring home a guest. He was a new Japanese friend they had just met on the street, and they hoped
it would be all right with me.

"You mean to spend the night?" I asked. "Because it's
almost midnight now."

"He has no stay place. Only the street."

"He'll have to sleep in the meditation room."

"Is that okay to you?"

"Sure, I guess. Just for tonight."

"But I think he wants to live with us."

It was a surprising idea, all of a sudden. They had met him
only this evening, and I had not even seen him. As they were
on their way across the bridge on the late bus from San
Francisco to Oakland, I sat in the meditation room. This was
a den as large as our living room. It had paneled walls and a
fireplace and a window that looked out on the living bamboo
fence that surrounded our backyard. On the floor, ceiling,
walls, and shelves were articles and artifacts that I had
brought back from my recent trip to India. There was a Bud-
dha, a puja table, and, almost always, burning incense. No

104

one had ever slept in here before, but now it would become another bedroom. This new friend would be joining our Japanese household, I was sure.

There had been a complete turnover in the population of the household since Tsutomu returned home to Sakai. For a short while I had lived alone in the original Berkeley flat. Then, before my departure for India, another group had gathered, and we had moved to this even larger place in Oakland. Eventually, through a number of friends returning to Japan, people began to hear about our place even before they left their country. Now we had a half-dozen people in a three-bedroom apartment, and Mitziko had a room to herself. She was our only female roommate. Mitziko had called our number several weeks ago at the recommendation of a mutual friend in Japan, but none of our people had known her.

Shozo and a couple of others went to meet her in a restaurant, and Shozo urged us all to accept her. "She is mainly a person, exactly same as us," he had said. "She is not joining as a woman, just as a person." So we had a full house now, and there was nowhere for this new addition to sleep except in the meditation room. It was not so strange after all, I realized, to be welcoming another stranger. I had met Tsutomu on the street. More than a couple dozen roommates had passed through our rotating household, and most of them I'd met by chance, or they had met me when they moved in.

I heard them removing their shoes at the front door and went to meet them. "This is Kari," Mitziko said. "We found him on the sidewalk. He played trumpet on the sidewalk to get money. But he couldn't get enough money for food. You know the Japanese restaurant near Chinatown Gate? That upstairs restaurant you went with us? He was at that sidewalk and he was hungry, so we had to get in the restaurant with him. Maybe he will stay with us. He doesn't have friends. Only us."

Kari and I looked at each other. "He doesn't know English," Shozo said.

Kari removed his stocking cap and simply stood with a

totally open expression, as though allowing me an opportunity to arrive at my own impression. He was young—perhaps about twenty. What was he doing here, I wondered, playing for coins on the streets of San Francisco? And how did he get here? He had no place, no money, no acquaintances, no English, and no possessions other than his trumpet. "He looks like a monk," I said. It could have been his calm, steady expression. Maybe something in his face reminded me of the monks I had seen in the temples of Japan and Korea.

"It's correct," Mitziko replied. "How do you know? He had been a monk in Japan."

"But he doesn't know how to play trumpet," Shozo added. "It sounds not too good, so he cannot get money. Do you want to hear it? It's something funny." We decided to wait until morning.

Several days passed before I heard Kari play. He was reluctant to blow his trumpet in the house, and I was even more reluctant to let him try it outdoors in our quiet neighborhood. There was a party one evening at which more than a dozen of our Japanese friends had gathered, and Kari was persuaded to perform. He stood in the middle of the room with his dark blue knitted stocking cap pulled down over his face so that only his chin was visible under the mouthpiece of his trumpet. Shozo had been right: he was no musician. It must have taken some amount of practice to produce these clear notes and to sustain them for so long; but he knew no music, and after we had heard the same few notes played in varying sequence to the point of monotony, someone requested him to stop. There was not a chance that he could earn a living as a Bay Area street musician.

"Now you can understand why he always wears his cap," Shozo told me. "Even on the street he plays with face covered."

The following day, Shozo, Mitziko, Kari, and I set out in Shozo's van for a drive along the coastal highway. They had arranged this opportunity to "have a special meeting," as they put it, "about Kari's situation."

106

"Maybe you can know he's a little bit crazy," Shozo said. "We have to find out how can we help him." He and Mitziko felt responsible, since they were the ones who had adopted Kari and brought him home. Now they were concerned about him and wanted my help. "Don't worry about our talking. We can talk anything we want because he doesn't understand. Anyway, he wants that we discuss about him now."

"I think he's not crazy," Mitziko said. "It's a different case than to be crazy."

"But he said he's crazy. He believe it himself."

"I know. So we have to help him understanding himself. He worries that he is crazy, but I think it's a kind of spiritual. He doesn't fit to usual society."

Shozo and Mitziko had spent a good deal of time with Kari, and now, during our scenic drive, while Kari sat quietly in the back seat, I learned more about him than I could have guessed from my limited observations. During the several days he had been with us, Kari had literally astounded Mitziko and nearly terrified Shozo. He had consistently intuited their thoughts and feelings and had spoken them aloud. He had described to them their own pasts—and even something of their futures—and had lectured them in detail about nature and the cosmos. They had come to regard him as a young man with some special knowledge or talent who was somewhat strange and troubled. He had no identification, no return ticket to Japan, and no money; and he claimed that he could not explain how he had arrived in the United States. He had no idea how he had come by his trumpet, or why he had no other belongings. Yet he was receiving his teachings, he said, from voices he was hearing inside his head.

Mitziko had studied philosophy, religion, and yoga in Japan and had been part of a group that had translated many classical metaphysical works into Japanese. Whatever were her own beliefs, her exposure was vast, and to her, Kari was an interesting challenge. But Shozo had been a salesman in a large Japanese corporation, and he had found Kari more disquieting than intriguing.

107

Kari had confided in his new friends—who he said were the first people he had ever spoken to about himself—and implored them to help him. He had studied philosophy and martial arts in a temple in Japan, where he had been living as a monk. His father, a successful businessman, had insisted that he leave the temple and prepare to join him in his business. He felt disoriented outside of the temple, and his father and other family members became increasingly oppressive in their attempt to make him change. Kari decided he was a hopeless misfit, and he longed to escape. Now that he was here in America, he wanted his friends to find him a psychiatrist or someone who could "cure" him. If he could be helped, he could then decide whether he wished to return to his family and the business or to his mountain temple.

A psychiatrist was not the answer, I was sure—not unless we could find an unconventional Japanese psychiatrist who could appreciate Kari's background and understand his language and who would need no fee. I thought of a better idea. "I think we have to find a Japanese monk to talk to Kari," I told them. "There are several in this area." They agreed, and so did Kari.

Only days later, we were on our way to the southern part of the peninsula to visit Kobun Chino at his home. Kobun Chino was a Zen roshi who had played a major role in the founding of the Tassajara Zen Monastery and the introduction of Zen in the West. I had met him once at a conference sponsored by the Association for Transpersonal Psychology. He was a young and mild-mannered man, but he was regarded as an influential elder—even by some of the elders in his own lineage.

He stepped out into his front yard to greet us as we pulled up. I was prepared to remind him of our previous meeting, but he seemed to recognize me immediately. I was also prepared to explain to him why we had come to seek his help—though I was not sure how best to go about it—but I soon discovered that he did not want or need an explanation. Our appointment had been arranged by Sonja Margulies, who was herself a Zen priest. She was a longtime family friend who had studied under Kobun Chino and was ordained by him. If she had explained anything to him, it could not have been more than what little I had told her. She had simply arranged our meeting time and then called back to give directions. Beyond our introductions and a few words of greeting, there was mostly silence as he sat us down on his living-room floor and knelt beside us to prepare tea, right there at the table.

He poured hot water from a larger pot into a tiny teapot to steep the tea. It took awhile to steep, and several repetitions to fill all the cups. It had felt strange at first to be sitting with these friends while a robed priest prepared our tea. But it was a ritual, I realized, and an important one for our meeting. After only a few minutes of this quiet and meticulous procedure, I began to feel extremely calm. Many sentences had been racing through my head. I'd had a slight sense of urgency and even a bit of apprehension as to whether our host would find our visit appropriate—I had not been at all aware of these until I felt them fading away. I began to feel as though I could sit through the entire afternoon, or even the week, simply having tea.

Kobun Chino then conversed with Kari, while the rest of us sat quietly. Shozo and Mitziko understood the conversation but offered no comments, and I simply watched and listened to the sounds. Kari did most of the talking, and though I could not understand his words, it seemed by his manner and his tone that he was being eloquent. He may have been merely explaining his situation, but Shozo and Mitziko appeared very impressed.

The roshi put up his hand and nodded. "Perhaps it is purposeful that he came to this country," he said, turning to me. "This one seems to have reached a level of advancement in his previous lifetimes, and now, in his new circumstances, he has forgotten who he is. In these past years he has awakened only partially—only enough to arouse the chi energy and intuition that he had developed in the past, but without the accompanying awareness. There may be others like him in his generation. I was thinking about Tassajara because

109

sometimes the total environment of a place like Tassajara can be sufficient to jog the memory of such a one and get him back on track. It is a sad fact in my country, but those who wish to remain totally and without distraction on the Zen path or who wish to sustain some traditions of their Oriental ancestors will find this easier in the West now and more difficult in Japan."

Again he spoke to Kari.

"Just now Tassajara is having their retreat," he went on, "and there will be a large group of Westerners. It would not be appropriate at this time. Rather than to wait, I thought perhaps I could be helpful in arranging for him to stay for a time at the Zen Center in San Francisco. I have explained this to him, and he is in agreement. I will see what I can do."

When arrangements were completed, we took Kari to San Francisco. With the help of his new friends, he had accumulated a few articles of clothing and toiletries, and so now he carried a small suitcase in addition to his trumpet. Shozo had tried to pursuade him to leave the trumpet behind, but Kari could not be sure when or whether he would ever be returning. The three of us were offered a guided tour of the Zen Center, but Kari did not accompany us. He was whisked away upon our arrival and taken to his quarters. He would get his own orientation. Shozo and Mitziko were saddened to see him taken away, and they wondered aloud whether he would be all right.

"Anyway, I promised him we will visit whenever he wants," Shozo told me as we were leaving. "And I told him he should not play his trumpet in the Zen Center."

Several days had to pass before we could visit. This was according to the rules, for upon his admission to the Zen Center, Kari had to make the necessary commitments and agree to follow the traditional procedures. The day of our visit was his first day of freedom from a very restricting regimen, and Kari wanted to go out and walk around. His free time was limited, but we had a couple of hours to walk around the neighborhood and to sit on a wall at the top of the street to talk. He was happy to see his friends and wanted

110

to share his past days with us—or with them—for he could not tell it in my language.

It was a very emotional telling. Kari shed tears openly as he talked, and Shozo and Mitizko seemed close to tears as they listened. They offered me an occasional few words of explanation, and I learned that Kari had been weeping frequently during meditations and times of silence. It was not a mournful weeping, he had told them, but an automatic response to his very wonderful feelings of opening and remembering. In any case, this had caused him some difficulties in the center, and he had been told repeatedly that he must not allow himself such emotional distractions during meditation. Kari was explaining his experiences in depth and evoking a very intense response from both of them.

When his time with us was up, we left him on the front steps of the Center, assuring him that we would remain in touch. For a long while, we rode in silence. Then Mitziko, still visibly moved, attempted to convey to me the sense of his communication. His situation was different from that of the others there, she felt, and she doubted whether they could really understand him. In any case, she could not see how he could do what he was there to do and not experience any emotion. She told me something of his memories and his visions and of how he had described why these had made him weep. From her words it sounded to me as though Kari, in all his quiet moments, felt the presence of the Divine Mother in Her most benevolent form—or felt himself to be in Her presence. His only longing was to sustain his sense of that loving presence: it was his only enduring and assuring continuity. But it was not Kari's personal experience that had so moved the two of them. It was what they had felt in him through his telling. "His soul is so much beautiful," she said. "I never saw something like him during my whole life."

A few more days passed, and we were talking of driving over the bridge to visit Kari again when the Zen Center called. Kari would have to leave. They could not allow him to stay there any longer. The caller was an English-speaking Westerner—an American monk or priest, I supposed, who appeared to be in charge. He politely and carefully explained to me that Kari's circumstance was a very special one and presented problems which were not the fault of anyone but which neither he nor this particular center were at all equipped to handle.

"Today he hit one of our people here," the man reported. "He didn't hurt him, but he did strike him. I've had Kari here in my office and we've talked about it. In fact, I've offered that if Kari had any further need, I would be willing to let him hit me. I'm not judging that Kari was in the wrong. I understand why he did what he did. I can see some purpose in it beyond usual appearances; but, as I've said, we just are not the right place for Kari. The program here and the other participants do not provide the right environment to support his particular purpose. If you want me to, I'd be more than willing to contact—"

"No, no," I said. "It's all right. I fully understand."

"Then can you agree to take him back today?"

I agreed, and though Shozo and Mitziko were sorry for what had happened, they were pleased that he'd be coming home.

Jiro, another member of our household, was not so happy at Kari's return, and he scolded him gruffly the moment we got him in the door. Jiro was smaller than Kari, but several years older, and much more practical—and wiser, in his own view. He'd received extensive training in martial arts and acupuncture and had trained himself in music, gymnastics, and creative dance and was giving performances around the Bay Area. At first he had tried to help Kari but had soon given up and lost interest in him. As an aikido student himself, he had found Kari's confusions simply annoying, and now the news of his having hit an American Zen aspirant was too much to tolerate. But Kari only smiled at Jiro's reprimanding and responded in such a gentle manner that now Jiro looked confused, and he left the room, apparently totally disarmed.

I asked Shozo what Jiro had said.

"He said he wants to hit Kari now because Kari hit somebody. He is a kind of brother in same training and he made shame to Jiro and all their people because he forgot his discipline."

"What did Kari say?"

"He gives praise to Jiro. And he agreed. It's a kind of thank you to Jiro. I think Jiro surprised to see such a thing from Kari. Kari didn't say it to change Jiro's mind. He just expressed his really feelings."

I discovered, somewhat by accident, that Kari could understand me when I spoke to him in English. I knew a few words of Japanese and could make some simple sentences, and Kari had by now picked up a few words of English; but I wanted to communicate with him beyond the simple exchanges we could make with our limited vocabularies. I knew we had to deal with his situation and make some positive changes, and I often tried to communicate with him through Shozo or Mitziko. Each time I tried this, Kari would capture them in a long, involved discussion that went on in its own direction. Mitziko would be moved and inspired and Shozo, awestruck; but in terms of plans and arrangements, we never got anywhere. So once when I found him alone in the house, I sat him down on the sofa, and I began to talk.

Kari only watched me with his usual gentle and open expression, and I went on, telling him in English that I hoped he could intuit my meaning as he had intuited so much else. It was time, I said, for him to put aside for a while his recurring memories, his unusual psychic gifts, and even his inner experiences, and to come up with some practical ideas for himself. Unless he could begin to participate in some practical planning, there was no way we could help him. He had to try to be something close to normal. He was upsetting Jiro and frightening Shozo, and he had disturbed our downstairs neighbors by sitting in the furnace room and pounding on the pipes. "It's just not right to freak people out," I said. "You may know what you're doing, but you have to think of others. You have to at least attempt to fit in, wherever you are. It's your responsibility. You have to choose where you want to

113

be and then try to behave appropriately in the place of your choice."

I looked at him. There was no way he could have understood and no way he could respond. It occurred to me how strange I must have looked and sounded to him, rattling off in English, knowing he could not understand. I myself was acting crazy—even while I was lecturing about appropriate behavior. Kari laughed and patted me on the shoulder.

"Understand," he said.

I had to reflect for a moment. Had he understood the meaning of my words, or was he telling me not to worry about how I looked to him? Again he patted me on the shoulder. "Kari, are you picking up my thoughts?"

"Yes," he said.

"Do you understand my words when I speak English?"

"No."

That was a surprising response. "Then are you reading my mind?"

"Yes," he said, pointing to his temple. He put his hand over my mouth and tapped his temple again. Then he touched my forehead.

Either I had read his mind or his gesture was very effective. He wanted me to communicate telepathically, without speaking. I closed my eyes and pondered. I wondered what to "say," or how I could tell whether he understood. I could ask him a question, but he could not answer. Perhaps I could give him some simple instruction and see whether he did what I "told" him to do. I realized I was about to test his psychic powers. Now it seemed he was once again in control. I had just appealed to him to forget about his psychic gifts for a while, and now he was engaging me in observing them.

As I sat with my eyes closed, I became aware of a tightness and a steady, burning pain in the back of my neck. It was only from tension in my eyes, I realized. I had been lying out in the sun on the roof of our garage and, against my better judgment, had neglected to cover my eyes.

"Good!" Kari exclaimed, patting the floor between his feet. "Okay, okay. Massage."

114

"Massage" is a word most Asians know, along with a variety of effective techniques—and I had learned the word "amma," which worked both in Korea and Japan whenever "massage" did not. I was always a willing recipient, even when I was not in need. But now I was in need, and I was appreciating his helpful offering. Kari's telepathy, if that is what it was, was serving a useful purpose.

As I sat on the floor in front of him while he worked on my neck and shoulders, I became aware of my thoughts. I was trying to think of what I could say to the others to bring about a focused meeting that would lead to some decisions. I realized this was not the time for such internal dialogue. It was not appropriate to the treatment, for one thing, and if Kari had intuited my thoughts before, he could certainly be doing it now.

For several minutes I held in my mind an image—or concept—which I felt would be familiar to Kari. I tried to contemplate a female or motherlike entity such as Kari had experienced during his meditations in the Zen Center. Even this contemplation was merely a thought process at first. While Kari pressed, almost painfully at times, on certain points along my neck and shoulders, I considered the possibility that the concept of the Divine Mother must be common to all cultures—possibly a universal archetype to which any human mind could attune. This archetype could encompass all the images of caring, nurturing, and motherhood, as well as the concept of the Earth Mother. The symbol of the Mother meant tolerance and unconditional love, and the concept of motherhood suggested family in the widest sense, the principle of the relationship of all life. It occurred to me that if one could actually be in such a presence, one could be with anyone or everyone. This could provide the ultimate device, if one could call it that, for communicating with anyone.

"So desu!" Kari exclaimed in Japanese.

Then I felt that I saw Her. My internal thoughts and dialogue ceased, and I felt that Kari and I were simply sitting in front of this mother being—and She was looking at us. At

115

the same time, I remained aware of myself sitting on my living room floor with Kari on the sofa behind me. In my image, we only looked at Her, and there were no words or thoughts until I felt myself hoping that Kari was seeing this, also. Then I began to wonder whether this was Kari's image or mine, and suddenly I spoke aloud: "Is this my experience," I asked Her, "or is it Kari's, also?"

"This is my experience," She said.

Kari's hands were still on me, and as they began to tremble, I could sense that he was shaking. I moved away and looked at him. Tears were running down his cheeks.

"I know," he said.

For a long while we sat in silence, but Kari wanted to go on. "English speak!" he said. I felt I had lost interest in my original topic, and I could think of nothing else to say. If he were able to speak English, or I, Japanese, I would have wanted to talk about what had just happened. "English speak!" he repeated.

"Why should I speak English?" I said. "You can't understand it, and if you can pick up my thoughts, why should we use any language?"

He looked at me blankly.

"Okay," I said, "if you can understand what I'm saying now, then pretend you just heard someone on the front porch and so you go to look out the door."

He closed his eyes, and after a moment, he said, "Nekko!"

It meant cat, I knew. "Did you understand me?" I asked.

He got up, walked into the foyer, and pointed out through the glass door. I got up to look. There was a cat curled up on our doormat. He pointed at it and tapped his temple, as he had done before, and the cat jumped up abruptly and looked at us through the glass. "Nekko massage," Kari said, and he held out his hands and wiggled his fingers. I could clearly see waves of ripples on the cat's back. It flopped down on the porch, rolled onto its back, and stretched out its front paws. Then, as though startled, it jumped up and started to dart away. Kari shouted "Stop!" and the cat stopped. It sat on the top step and looked in at us. I could see it meow, but we could hear nothing through the door. Kari waved his hand in a motion of dismissal. "I am sorry," he said.

Kari reached for my arm to pull me away, and I sensed that he wanted to let the cat be, but then he fell to his knees, nearly pulling me down with him. I tried to help him up, but he did not want me to touch him. Finally he stood and walked slowly into the living room. Jiro came in the back door and walked in through the kitchen in time to see Kari staggering about.

"What's the matter with him?"

"I don't know," I said.

Jiro reached for him, and Kari stepped back, bumping into a planter. He nearly knocked it over. Angrily, Jiro grabbed the front of his collar and twisted, holding him tight. "What's the matter with you?" he shouted in English and then in Japanese. "This is not necessary thing!" Jiro said to me. "Anybody could get deep vision and big emotion. He's a kind of overacting. He suppose to control himself!" Kari just stood there with his usual neutral expression. "Are you proud to yourself?" Jiro shouted in English.

I could sympathize with Kari, and this was uncomfortable to see. Yet, I felt it might be helpful. Kari held up his hands and said something, and Jiro let go of him. Kari went on talking—so softly I could hardly hear his voice. Then he sat down on the floor and looked away, and Jiro turned toward me. I was surprised to see that now Jiro had tears. "Anyway, I think he is not usual people. It's a problem. Outside is something crazy and inside is gentleman. But his mind is so good. You know? Sometimes he just touched to our heart."

We all agreed that Kari should not continue to stay with us. We could go on sheltering him indefinitely, and it would only postpone what he was trying to resolve. After some checking around, we decided that the Berkeley YMCA might be suitable for Kari, and Kari seemed to be agreeable to whatever we decided. The Berkeley Y always had a number of traveling visitors from Japan, and even some employees spoke Japanese. It would be relatively inexpensive, together we could manage it, and there was a possibility that Kari could work there and earn some income. Even though Shozo had been so bewildered by him, he was the most reluctant to arrange for Kari's departure. It was as though we were repeatedly trying to get rid of him, and Shozo would have been willing to go on caring for him.

Jiro felt this step might be even more useful than a temple arrangement, at least for a time. "He has to learn how to be a human being," Jiro said. "If we stop protecting him, he is forced to be normal. Then his spirit will help him. Then he can find his own temple—whatever he wants."

Shozo and Mitziko planned to meet with him that evening while I was out. It was supposed to be a meeting to discuss arrangements and to induce Kari to begin to think practically. "I don't want to happen anything spiritual," Shozo had said, but it turned out otherwise. I came home after midnight to find the three of them sitting in the living room, appearing as though they were in a trance. It took much urging on my part to get even a slight response from them. In the middle of the floor sat a calico cat, one I had never seen before—and it also appeared to be in a trance.

"Where did this cat come from?" I asked. No one answered. "It's not ours, so we should let it out." I picked it up and put it out on the porch. "Why did you have that cat in here?" I asked again, trying to induce them to speak.

"Kari made it," Shozo said. "Just here it became to be a cat." He was visibly shaken.

"Materialize," Mitziko said. "You know?"

"Well, it didn't just materialize," I said. "It came in here from somewhere."

"No," Mitziko said, in a matter-of-fact tone. "We saw it."

I found myself checking for an open door or window as if to disprove them. But we had screens on all the windows and self-closing screens on the doors. "Well, Kari somehow called it," I asserted, remembering the other cat, "but he did

118

not materialize it. Anyway, forget it. I want to know about your plans."

But there was no response. They did not want to talk. "I'm okay," Mitziko said at last. "But Shozo is confused."

I helped Shozo to his feet. "Can I talk to you?" he said. We went into his room to talk, but he only sat on his bed and trembled and could not make himself talk.

I tried to think of what to do. There was a twenty-four-hour delicatessen nearby, and it occurred to me that it would help him to get out into the fresh air and to be among people in a public place. "Let's go get a milkshake," I said, "and in a little while you'll feel okay again." He agreed. We looked in through the window of the delicatessen, but Shozo was too shaken to go inside, so we went on. As we walked, he repeatedly asked me whether I could see him, and I assured him that I could. He told me that he had come to see that he did not really exist, and this was terrifying to him.

"If you don't exist, you could not feel frightened," I said. "You wouldn't feel anything."

"But Kari explained this body is only imagine. Before in the house I disappeared. I didn't know if I could come back."

"Look, it's the whole nonsense about that cat that got you so shook up. Forget about it. It was just a cat."

"Did you see it?"

"Of course I saw it, I put it outside. And it didn't materialize. It's just a cat from somewhere in the neighborhood. Somehow it got in."

"No, you are wrong. There was made some sparks and then only orange color like a piece of smoke. Then it came to be a cat. We watched it. I never saw like that happen, but I believe it."

"Well, believe it or not, it was silly," I said, trying to discount it, more for him than for me. "There was no sense in doing that."

"Anyway, you don't understand. He showed us that all this is not real, it just only looks like."

"Even if it just looks like it, you can see me, right? And I can see you. Of course things aren't what they look like.

THE MONK FROM THE PAST

They're not what they look like, because they're so much more. You're not less than you imagine, you're more than you imagine."

"But I became afraid that I might disappear."

"Is that why you asked me if I could see you? Do you want me to let you know if you disappear?" He thought for a moment about what I'd said, and fortunately, it struck him funny and he chuckled. "See? Whatever Kari did or said—it might be true. But it's not scary to think about it, it's just funny. People don't just disappear, and you can't disappear just because you listened to Kari." Shozo soon felt real enough, and hungry enough, to have that milkshake after all.

◐   ◐   ◐

We moved Kari into the YMCA. Shozo continued to have mixed feelings. He still felt as though we were getting rid of him and subjecting him to greater hardship, but he certainly did not want to experience him any further. Kari actually seemed to fare better than Shozo. There were a few episodes in which Kari "read" the minds of the employees or came down from his room to the front desk to describe to them what they had just been doing. Someone called me once to say she could not handle his being there, and I was afraid we were once again back where we had started. But then she called me back to say that she had changed her mind. Too many others had wanted him to stay, and she had decided that although he was strange, he was also unique and interesting, if you could take him "with a grain of salt." Fortunately, I realized, she and the others were far too busy to experience one of Kari's in-depth lessons.

Shozo, on the other hand, struggled for several weeks, especially at night. He moved into my room and placed his mat beside my bed, and he reached up and poked me again and again throughout the night, so that I would wake up and assure him that he had not disappeared. But for explanations, he began to turn to Mitziko, who could speak his language. She had been intrigued but not so bewildered by Kari, and she seemed to be familiar with all kinds of phenomena that Shozo now felt forced to think about. They began to spend all their free time together and eventually announced their engagement. Not long afterward they were married.

Kari simply disappeared. We saw him occasionally during the next several weeks and were reassured to find signs of his fitting in. He began to earn his own living teaching young people in the gym. He bought a bicycle, learned his way about, and took care of his own errands. During that time, my sister Sandra was a part-time swimming instructor for children at the Y and occasionally saw Kari. She told me of an astounding demonstration he had made with his bicycle. He had often left it unattended outside the building, for which he was cautioned by the others. Bicycle theft abounded in the area—even locked bicycles had often been stolen. Kari had explained that he had arranged for protection for his bike, and to demonstrate the fact, he had placed his bicycle hanging halfway off the curb in downtown Berkeley's busiest intersection and left it overnight. The next day they went to find it undisturbed in that very spot—where now cars had to swerve to avoid running over the wheel.

My sister was there one rainy night when Kari put on his jacket and stocking cap and wheeled his bicycle through the lobby. Everyone insisted that it was raining too hard for him to ride, but he said that it was time for him to say goodbye, and that since it was time, the weather did not matter. He went down the steps, through the front door, and out into the rain. Everyone expected he would soon be back, drenched and resolved to wait—but neither they nor any of us nor any of our friends ever saw him again.

◗   ◗   ◗

I supposed Kari got back to Japan somehow. I would have liked to have seen him again. I thought about him from time to time. I cared about what might become of him, and I was curious. I believed what the roshi had said: what Kari really needed was recollection. His brain had forgotten who he was. I would have liked to have known him when it remembered.

While I was still living in the area, a friend and I attended a

*lecture at a private institute. The guest speaker was a thera-
pist at a large hospital in San Francisco who, with the help of
some colleagues, was conducting his own independent out-
of-body research project. That was what he called it, but it
sounded to me more like a campaign than a research project. He seemed to be so personally angered at the materialistic, flesh-only view that he was determined to induce
everyone he could get his hands on (or his apparatus on) to
get out there and see for themselves.*

*We heard about his forceful methods for inducing people
out of their bodies and about some of the episodes reported
by his subjects. It was an intense process, it seemed to me,
almost harsh—as though drastic measures were in order to
force a change in the prevailing view. Literally everyone, he
claimed, must be helped to this important revelation.*

*My friend had spent years working with young people who
had had disturbing experiences with LSD and other psyche-
delics, and he had had some experience himself with a wide
range of altered-state inducers. He was amazed at this
speaker's sense of urgency about his cause and the lengths
to which he was willing to go. "Out-of-body?" he whispered
to me. "He's pushing out-of-body? Give me twenty-four
hours and I can bring him a couple dozen people who could
use some help staying in. Where's this guy been?"*

*The term "out-of-body" is likely to be misleading to some
people. One is not, after all, waiting inside one's body like a
genie in a bottle. It is one's attention, one's focus, that is
either "in" or "out"—either here or there. "All of the body is
in the mind—not all of the mind is in the body," as Swami
Rama said. The physical body is in the etheric body and the
etheric body is in the astral body—and all of the body is in
the mind.*

*A young student I knew attended some seminars in which
many of the participants discussed their various out-of-body
experiences. Apparently, he sensed their pride in their
achievement and began to feel somewhat left out—or left in,
as the case may be. He made a few unsuccessful attempts
and soon became discouraged. "I wish I could have an out-*

of-body experience," he complained to me. "I've tried and I can't do it."

"Of course you can," I told him. "You do it all the time. You do it in your sleep."

"Well, how come I can't remember it?"

"You do remember. You can't do something and not remember it."

"No, I really don't remember."

"This is just your brain talking, making sentences when it doesn't know what it's talking about. Who asked your brain? Of course your brain can't remember?"

"Why can't my brain remember?"

"Why should it? Your brain wasn't there. You can't go out of your body and take your brain along."

"Some people remember. I've heard people talk about it. They describe it when they're awake."

"But they don't ask their brains, they tell their brains. Brains don't know anything, they're just receivers with switchboards. Train your brain to be receptive—not to talk but to listen—and maybe it will hear whatever it's told."

The left brain is talking all the time. It has something to say about everything. It calls itself a rational faculty and it thinks itself reasonable. Yet, when it is in no position to interpret an experience in which it cannot even participate, it tries. It has something to say about everything. The brain has no way to gather information—it just talks. Information must be introduced from without. When information is lacking, the brain says, "No it wasn't, no I didn't, no there aren't."

But with methods such as were described in the lecture, or with the many drugs my friend knew about, it is possible to dull the roar of the brain without inducing unconsciousness and thus subject it to the imput it would not normally receive. If this can be achieved in a voluntary and controlled manner, it can serve some purpose. Out-of-body training and practice has been useful in many cases with prisoners or paraplegics, for example. It is not the experience that is unusual, in any case. It is unusual when the brain is let in on it.

123

◐   ◐   ◐

In my mind I sometimes contemplate the little diagram that Jay made for me with his finger as we sat on the floor in his father's farmhouse: two circles with a bridge between. Sometimes I imagine walking back and forth across the bridge. It goes from the world of matter into the world of mind. It goes from the world of explanation to the world of knowing, from the rational to the intuitive, from objective observation to subjective sensitivity. I imagine walking back and forth between two very different but equally familiar realms—but finding each of them familiar only when I am there. It is easy to see how someone could simply deny the existence of the other side. From the rational side, the intuitive realm cannot readily be seen, and one who denies its existence is not likely to try the bridge.

It is usual to wake up and forget what we have been doing. It is usual, in fact, to be born and forget where we have been. What if we pass on and forget that we were here? Most people expect to remember. Some expect repentance, reparation, or reward; but most expect at least to remember. Think how many people conceptualize and contemplate the infinite hereafter without giving any thought to the herebefore—as though one could have hold of a stick that is infinitely long —but only on one end. Not many people expect to remember where they have been. For Kari, it would have been helpful to remember, for he had brought with him a level of advancement that he had developed in the past, but without the accompanying awareness.

Kari felt disoriented outside of the temple. "In his new circumstances," as the roshi had put it, "he has forgotten who he is." He had brought the chi energy and the intuition that he had developed in the past—so he could manifest all those phenomena—but there was no continuity. Kari, like the old farmer, was on both sides of the bridge; but he was only partially aware on the side that was visible to those around him. He had lost the connecting threads of his contexture.

In the new culture—either here or in Japan—Kari was out of context, and "there may be others like him in his generation." There may be others who have "reached a level of advancement in a previous lifetime," as the roshi put it, and have forgotten, in their new circumstances, who they are. There may not be many just like Kari, but there are many who are quite out of context in modern cultures, both East and West. There are many, particularly among the youth, who have come into their new lives to find themselves out of context—like lost persons in a social wilderness. What will provide the special contextual support that is needed to help them?

Rolling Thunder told me that when a doctor "sees the sickness and not the man . . . it certainly isn't healing." We say that holistic healing recognizes more than the carcass and seeks to treat "the whole person"—body, mind, and spirit. But what is truly holistic—truly healing—is to treat the whole person in context. Traditional medicine people in their healing rituals attend less to their patients' manifest conditions than to their patients' circumstances. Rolling Thunder would say that to treat the sickness one must treat the context in which it occurs. But what can be done for one who is out of context? What can be done to "jog the memory of such a one and get him back on track"? We don't generally acknowledge or even recognize a problem such as "out of context." When Rolling Thunder told me about finding the girl whose body lay "empty" in the hospital, it struck me how much vital knowledge and understanding has been lost in the process we've called "progress"—knowledge that once was commonplace. "You people don't even know what a human being is," he had said. "You can look right at someone's empty body and think that you're lookin' at the person when they're not even there." We need to remember and to regain the capacity to see what Rolling Thunder knows to be "just natural to see." Just as it is important to recognize when one has lost track of one's body, it is crucial to be able to see when one has lost track of one's contexture.

In spite of all that had been said about not protecting him and forcing him to be "normal," my hope was that Kari had found some temple with an appropriate circumstance for him. Self-integration needs an appropriate context, and Kari needed to return to the realm in which he had become who he was in the first place.

It was good to have known him—good for all of us. Even Jiro had said, "He just touched to our heart." I continue to return to the image of Kari sitting in the presence of the Mother. I remember hearing Her say, "This is my experience." One can return to such an image whenever one wishes. It is a universal reality. She is always there—but we seem not to be—and when we "return" to Her, we wonder how we could have "forgotten" Her. Kari spoke of seeing Her —always in his meditations.

I thought of Kari from time to time—in the living room with me, or in some temple, or talking with our friends. When he sensed Her presence, he wept. It happened again and again. Through him, others caught some glimpse and said, "His soul is so much beautiful. But it is everyone's beauty. From time to time everyone sees the Mother—and everyone says, "How could I have forgotten you? How could I have turned away—even for a moment?" And She answers, "No, you have been here with me. I am holding you always and never lose sight of you."

SCENE SEVEN

Henry and
Joseph Himself

I met Henry Paradise near the Duck Valley Indian Reservation in Idaho. Henry was a Shoshone, but he was not, by anyone's reckoning, a medicine man. He was, by all appearances, however, an Indian. He had a picturesque face, with plump cheeks and cheerful eyes. He spoke Shoshone and Piute, and his English, though his Indian accent sounded familiar, was unlike anything I had ever heard.

But it was not because he was an Indian that it was arranged for me to meet him. In fact, I did not travel to Idaho to see Henry the Indian. I went to talk with—or, perhaps, listen to—Joseph. Joseph was another aspect of the same being. Joseph spoke through Henry, using Henry's brain and mouth, his limited English, and his Indian accent; but Joseph made it clear that he was no Indian. Such physical traits —or, to Joseph, such secondary and temporary traits—as race were unrelated to Joseph's identity.

Henry had once traveled, at Joseph's behest, to the Southern Peninsula in the San Francisco Bay Area, where he met with directors of the Academy of Parapsychology and Medicine. This was part of an urgent search, which apparently

127

had been left up to Henry and which had taken him over thousands of miles in several states. It was Henry's responsibility, Henry claimed, to find listeners and interpreters for Joseph's message.

I first heard about Henry while I was back in Topeka helping set up the Kansas headquarters of the Cross-Cultural Studies Program. Bob Mattson and Marshal Spangler of the Academy contacted me by telephone, told me about their visit from Henry Paradise, and gave me his address and telephone number in Idaho. They thought I might perhaps be willing to be such a listener, but nearly two years passed before I was able to see Henry. Activities in Topeka were keeping me engaged. The Cross-Cultural Studies Program was set up as a tax-exempt organization to receive grants for intercultural research and communication and to promote understanding and respect for traditional peoples and their ways. If something were to be arranged with Henry—or Joseph—it would have to be as a project of the program, but I was not sure how relevant such a field investigation would appear to a prospective funder.

Once when I was in the Bay Area, I met with Marshal Spangler in a hotel lobby near San Mateo, and he gave me copies of tape recordings that had been made during Henry's visit to the Academy. Later I listened to the tapes—several times, carefully—but I found them difficult to understand. Though there were a few sentences which Henry claimed were spoken directly by Joseph, these tapes were, for the most part, recordings of Henry trying to explain to Bob and Marshal the meaning of Joseph's presence and the responsibility that this implied for Henry. Henry was accepting a burdensome task, and here he seemed to be struggling even to explain his situation.

I had three distinct impressions in listening to these tapes that captured my attention and made me want to help. For one thing, Henry was a recovered alcoholic who was poor and in poor health. He had little education, little background in the matters of which he tried to speak, and he was hardly articulate. But on the other hand, there were allusions to various philosophical doctrines and references that one would more likely hear from a scholar of metaphysics than from an old Indian off the reservation; while, at the same time, his words and manner indicated a sense of service and goodwill, of simple and humble caring that one would not likely hear from a dilettante of the occult. I realized that the humility and naiveté that could make it so easy to discount Henry entirely were the very factors that could be considered to validate his experience and his sense of purpose.

The first time I contacted Henry, I just happened to be nearby and thought it only fair that I should give him a call and perhaps drop in to say hello. I was visiting in Boise with Russ and Morning Star—longtime friends from my days with Rolling Thunder—and the three of us thought we might make the drive together. I made a phone call to Henry, who said, "Well, I've been expecting you for a pretty long time," and the three of us headed south for an afternoon visit.

Before we reached Henry's house, we stopped to spend a few minutes of silence on the bank of the Snake River. It was an unplanned stop: at a point where the paved road made a sharp uphill curve, a narrow dirt road went straight on through the trees and bushes. It must have looked inviting to Russ, for he drove straight ahead for the hundred yards or so that there was road, and the three of us got out and walked up to the river. None of us spoke nor even whispered. We just stood. It was one of the most silent places I had ever experienced. The only sounds were of birds and insects and the ripples in the river. Wild ducks and little birds walked about our feet. Morning Star knelt down beside a bird who was drinking from the river, and for a moment they were eye to eye. My companions were visibly moved, but no one spoke a word. Then we were on our way again. We did not speak until we were back on the pavement, and nothing was said about our enchanting interlude. I thought to myself that there must have been some reason for our having had those meditative moments at the river below Henry's cabin just prior to our meeting him. One benefit was the extraordinary degree of calm that we had realized. This, it turned out, was an important help in the challenge of being with Henry.

He was standing out in front when we pulled up. He may

129

have heard us coming, but he looked as though he had been standing there impatiently for hours. "I've been waiting for you for six years," he said to me as soon as I had introduced myself. "You folks come on in, and we've got to sit and talk."

I found myself hoping that he was not upset with me for having kept him waiting for six years, but I realized that only two years had passed since he had first heard my name during his meeting at the Academy of Parapsychology and Medicine. He had not been waiting especially for me. Yet, for six years he had been searching for someone to talk to—for anyone who would listen—and I could understand his very apparent anxiety. I felt a hint of anxiety myself, hoping that my appearing here did not seem to implicate some sort of promise or expectation that I could not fulfill.

He began his presentation even as we walked to the house and went in through the kitchen door, and his wife, who was standing just inside, reminded him that to be sufficiently hospitable, he should let us first sit down and be served our refreshments before he started in on us. So he forced himself to pause for a moment until we were sipping from tall glasses of iced tea, and then he went on:

"Now, I'm a human being and my name is Henry, Henry Paradise, member of Western Shoshone. I attended Indian school, only grade school, and trade school. So my trade is stonemason, and I don't have much education. I can't read or write too good, and so that's why we need somebody to help for that."

He paused and reflected for a moment. He looked anxious. Then he began again, and with a tone of urgency, as though this was now the moment for him to convince me or at least impress me: "My human mind is open to inner mind which is spirit mind which is open through me to the seventh sense level which is open to what is referred to as the spiritual counseling system for all the peoples all over the world for its own sake, and this is the gift that was received and produced and completed by the spirit counseling system which is the resurrection to arise your spirit mind to the fullest to receive the word just as quoted in the Bible which

130

is that in the beginning there was the word and the word was with God and it was the same inner being who has created the human form who is his child—and it is sound system, strictly sound vibration system which is the instrument that all human is created by their own god who is the true child of God and we are the child of our own creator who is the inner mind . . . so he always says to me that you are me and we are the same but to my human mind it always looks like two—"

"Of whom are you speaking?" I interrupted. "Who is it who says to you that you are the same? Are you referring to Joseph?" Generally, I was not inclined to interrupt; but his words were coming out in an endless stream, Russ and Morning Star were shifting uncomfortably in their chairs, and Henry seemed unable to stop. I thought I could perhaps get Joseph to speak.

"Well, I call him Joseph, that's what he said, because he has no form or image which could be given a name. The first time in the beginning I thought voices are coming somewhere in the room—somewhere outside. I used to look around—try to see what it is doin' the talking. Then I thought I'm going crazy. Maybe my drinking. I was drinking too much in those days. Alcohol problem. So he said. 'No, this is you, this is inside, not outside, and I am yourself.' That's what he said. 'I am your inner voice.' So we begin our conversation after that. It's just like when two people talk to each other. But he told me I am human so I will think it's two people, but it is only one. 'Well,' he says, 'you will never understand this, so you just go ahead and think like it's two—inner mind and outer mind.' This is the best pronouncement from the human side. He explained he has no image, no form, and no name."

"No name? So you just made up the name Joseph?"

"Yeah, that's in the beginning, in our conversation. Because he said there is no picture, no image to represent inner spirit. This is intangible, which human cannot understand. So he said, 'We make it easy for you because you are human, so you just call me Joe. I call you Henry, and you

131

call me Joe. That way we can talk to each other.' No, in fact, I did not make it up. He gave the name, the name is from him. So now I call him Joseph."

He went on with his story, and it appeared that he was much easier to understand when he was answering my questions than when giving his orations. Henry called himself a mutant. He claimed that his relationship with Joseph began after he was struck by an automobile and was nearly killed, and Joseph stepped in to bring him back. "When the seventh-sense level is slightly ajar," Henry explained, "the eighth-sense level can be opened up from the other side by the inner mind."

I remembered hearing on the tapes that Henry had called himself a mutant when he was talking with Bob and Marshal in California. I had thought that mutation was a change in a species produced by some marked effect upon the hereditary process, but I could see how Henry had chosen the word. He was trying to make the point that he was changed —a new and different person. I watched him sitting there, talking, coughing, and puffing on his cigarettes. I had no way of knowing how changed or new he was. But it seemed quite apparent that something interesting had happened to this man, something that spoke significantly about the arrangement of the selves.

He noticed that I was watching him smoke. "Now, these cigarettes, Joseph doesn't pay any mind to it, he says, but the drinking—that had to stop. Joseph told me the drinking could kill me next. I got struck by a car, and he brought me through that all right, so then he told me we gotta work on this drinking."

"So did you stop drinking?"

"Oh, yes. I don't drink no more. And I'm no alcoholic now. I can be around it, taste it, smell it, anything. I just don't relate to it no more. It's gone. He said I've gotta give that up if I want to live and also, he said, if I'm gonna talk to people. People might think I'm crazy anyway, so he says it's not gonna look too good if I'm a drunkard. So we had to overcome that. That was the most pronounced test of all to the

132

effect that I had forty days and forty nights of trial and tribulation completed in four states—California, Arizona, Utah,
and Nevada. This is the effectionated system used all
through the histories for the spiritual turnover of the change
ordered in coming to their understanding of the activated
movement to follow the golden rules of life."

Henry did indeed have a strange way of talking. He com-
bined his own colloquial vernacular with his awkward attempts at sophistication sufficient to speak for Joseph—or
about him. I knew that if Joseph, whoever he was, were to
speak through Henry directly—even if Henry were in a trance
—he would still be limited to the idiom that existed within
Henry's own brain. It seemed that Henry, needing language
and nuance that was not there, was doing his best to guess
at the appropriate wording. In any case, it seemed to go
better, at least at that moment, when Henry was doing the
talking and especially when we followed a sort of interview
format. Henry seemed to be clearer when relating his own
story than when trying to interpret Joseph's message.

We learned some of the details of Henry's forty-day "trial
and tribulation." The greatest ordeal, he told us, was the
running that he was instructed to do. He spent many days
and nights in a hotel in the Mission District in San Francisco,
and during this time, he ran for miles, up and down the hills.
It became especially difficult when he began to run barefoot.
He claimed that Joseph had made him invisible; but that
because Joseph was guiding him, or propelling him, in a
way that produced a loud clicking of his tongue, people were
turning their heads to look as Henry passed.

"It's your footsteps," Joseph told him. "Take off your
shoes and carry them, and no one will know you are a person."

"But my tongue," Henry complained. "My tongue is making a funny noise." He was able to simply think his sentences
to himself, and Joseph would respond.

"Just take off your shoes," was the reply, "and you will not
be noticed. People won't recognize the clicking sound, so
they will not pay attention."

133

If it were true, as Henry claimed, that he had run many miles, day and night, up and down the steep streets and sidewalks of San Francisco in his bare feet, he had indeed, for whatever cause or purpose, made a monumental effort. I gathered that all this work was essentially for the purpose of overcoming his dependency on alcohol.

One day, he admitted, he had a free ride in a taxicab. He had found himself too far from where he was staying and too exhausted to make it back—especially in his bare feet. Joseph suggested he ought to just take a taxi. Henry pointed out that there was nothing in his pockets—not even enough to ride a few blocks. "It's okay," Joseph assured him. "We'll put you in with someone going near your place, and you'll just share the ride. We'll hold up on your tongue clicking, and they won't even notice."

"Well, an old lady stopped a cab," Henry said. "Joseph gave the word and I just slid on in there—right beside her on the seat. No one looked at me. She stopped only a half-block from my place, paid the fare, and we got out. I never could figure that one out. I was s'posed to be invisible, but I opened the door for her when we got out and she never batted an eye!

"Well, when I was finally finished with all such kind of tribulations," Henry told us, "Joseph congratulated me. He says I'm free now, free from this part. So that's good, because that drinking, that would interfere with everything. Well then, I begin to think about my smoking, because I'm still smoking. I figured that's not gonna go over so good with Joseph."

"Are you planning to quit?" I asked. "And do you think Joseph will help you?"

"Well, Joseph told me, 'Maybe you just go ahead and smoke, because you're human.' He says, 'That drinkin' alcohol was a problem because it's gonna mess up the opening. That smoking's not going to do that.' So I said to Joseph, I said, 'Doesn't that bother you when I smoke?' You know what Joseph told me?"

"What?"

"Joseph said, 'No, it bothers you, Henry. It's not good for

134

you, but you smoke because you're human. Nothing bothers me because I don't have any form. I'm intangible.' Doug, can you, uh, do you follow this?"

"I think so," I said.

"So Joseph says to me that everything I enjoy personally, it don't mean much to him, one way or the other. He says everything he likes, I can't even imagine about that. Joseph told me not to worry about it too much at this time because someday it's all gonna be given up. I thought he was talking about the cigarettes, so I says, 'You mean my smoking?' and he says, 'No, I mean the human form.' Ain't that something?"

I agreed.

"Now Joseph has communicated this pronouncement that we don't have to think about the spirit world. That's their business—the spiritual counseling system. We're supposed to think about human business—to the effect of the qualification of the meaning of the human life—right here on this Earth. Then they will help us, too. That's the reason of the communication, and that's why you came here today. You can help, too, that's your job."

He looked at me pointedly and waited for my response. "I will try to arrange something," I said. There was not much else I could say.

It was difficult to leave—even after I repeatedly promised that I would try my best to come again and stay longer. Henry followed us out to the car, talking all the way, and telling us how important it was to hurry, because the message was urgent and time was limited. Then he waved us to a stop, even after we had started to drive away, and he ran up to my window for one last word: "Joseph says to tell you something when you try to make any arrangements. Joseph says to tell you that this is not an Indian project. The creator's concerns for human condition and happiness and the true spiritual boost for human life comes from intangible source not relation to any religion and not identification to any country or any race whatsoever. All the spiritual teaching is an absolutely free gift for anybody who's gonna use it for helping out. It is free for the asking, and it can come to any

135

listening post anywhere. There is no wisdom knowledge which goes to the human as a personal possession. And there is no spiritual teaching which is supposed to restrict to any human system or any identification requirements of race or ancestors. This is the most dangerous misunderstanding of human mind. Joseph says that this is very important to make it clear."

Those last words were indeed fortunate; for they were important to my own interest, and they appeared to be most significant to the people who encouraged me to explore this Henry-Joseph prodigy—and to those who eventually arranged for the necessary project funding.

I was not certain what needed to be done for Henry or for Joseph, nor how helpful I might be. Henry had spoken in his meeting with Bob and Marshal about some fireplaces he had built which he called "tablets." As a stonemason, Henry had constructed many fireplaces, but there were seven particular tablets whose stones had been selected by Joseph and whose measurements were to Joseph's specifications. Henry wanted mathematicians and other scientists, as he put it, to investigate these fireplaces for additional interpretation of Joseph's messages. I thought I could perhaps function as some sort of liaison for Henry, helping him to communicate with other listeners or investigators. "There is meaning in the shape and form itself," Henry had said. "It's geometry." Perhaps I could help him find someone to look at his fireplaces. People could take whatever interest they wished, or come to whatever conclusions; but at least I could help Henry make his requests.

I went back to Henry's place to talk with him about arrangements. If we could agree upon a time and place, and if I could learn how he, or Joseph, wished to proceed, I would move out to Idaho to spend every day—for several weeks, if necessary—listening, recording, taking notes, making contacts, whatever was needed. I had called Henry from Los Angeles, saying that I would be there the following day for a brief meeting to set up a game plan. So Henry was prepared for my arrival.

There was a rather professional-looking tape recorder set up on a shelf near our table and a microphone in front of Henry's chair. He had arranged for an acquaintance to bring this equipment because he had intended to prepare a recorded message for me to take back.

"We don't have much time right now," I said. "What I need to do here today is to make some plans. If you would like for me to spend some time with you, I'll be available, but I have to plan it in advance."

"Anytime is okay."

I knew we had to pin it down. It was my responsibility to make things exact. Suppose I should move out here to spend some weeks, only to find Henry away somewhere on his travels? I should not mind, really, having become somewhat accustomed to that sort of thing. But I should not likely be able to try again. Our opportunity would be gone—and owing to my own negligence. I took my calendar from my briefcase. I suggested beginning in November and going at least to the end of the year. "Let's see if we can make a six- to ten-week block of time—"

"We have to hurry up," Henry insisted. "I don't know nothing about your own religion. Maybe it's difficult for you to agree about Joseph's transmission and all such of concerns—"

"If it were a problem for me, I wouldn't be here, Henry. My own opinions are totally irrelevant—even to me. I can listen to you, talk to you, quote you, or write about you without regard to my own beliefs. That's my work—that's what I do—"

"Well, now, we're gonna send a message through you on, well, maybe one or two cassettes. We have to hurry up. So this can be used for listening by any doctors or scientists whatsoever, and all such references to the effect that—"

"No, Henry, I don't want to record." I knew it could not work. I would spend all day and then be on my way with one or two tapes with which I could do nothing, without any plans

137

or agreements, and that would be the end of it. "Let's arrange it now so that I can come back. Then we can record for hours and hours, day after day, if you want."

"That will be okay. But now, first, we'll record here like we prepared it here, and you're gonna have something concrete on the tape for the science investigation—"

"No, Henry." I felt certain and I had to sound definite. "We are not going to record today."

Henry lost his temper, and it was extremely startling. I was surprised at my own assertiveness and nearly frightened at what he might do. He slammed his fist down on the table. His face was crimson red. "Now, you just listen to me! Now, you're not gonna hold this off no longer! That's not your place to get in the way. I'm a old man, an' I'm gettin' weak, and we don't have enough time for you to be—"

He stopped abruptly and sat stone-still. His face paled and his eyes closed. For a moment I thought he might be having a stroke, but then there came a very different, very calm voice: "Henry, the man, as a human being, as all human beings, is defective. You have your defects, but impatience is not among them. It is assumed you have the capacity to tolerate Henry. Henry's lack of patience will not interfere while you maintain your own. The recording will occur later, as you have understood."

Henry pushed back his chair and opened his eyes. He glanced at me and then looked down. He lit a cigarette and stuck it tightly in his lips. Then his expression of discomfort faded. "It's lookin' good—gonna turn out pretty okay, I guess. I been waitin' for this and, uh, when you gonna come back?"

That was the first time I had heard Joseph so clearly and directly—the first time that it seemed certain it could not have been Henry. It was, in fact, the most striking example of an inner voice that I had ever heard—the most striking contrast, at least, that I had ever witnessed in one person.

The rest of the meeting went smoothly, and we did not record. We agreed upon a schedule. Henry would stay with his brother Charlie in a trailer park in Nampa, Idaho, and would be available to me for whatever time I could remain available to him. I left knowing that, at least, I had committed myself to some extensive and intensive recording sessions.

Jerry Cox, a young friend I had met in my workshops in Topeka, became a staff member of the Cross-Cultural Studies Program and a research assistant for this strange new project. Jerry and I flew to Phoenix, picked up a station wagon that had been donated for the duration of the project, and drove to Boise. We set up our "base camp" in an efficiency apartment in the Colony Motel in Boise. For weeks we drove from Boise to Nampa, nearly every day, and often on a snowy, icy highway that was treacherous and slippery.

It was exhausting work. The slow drive and the many hours of recording made the days drag on and on, and it did indeed take considerable patience to sit quietly as Henry went on and on, hour after hour, with his obscure and redundant dissertations. Jerry generally drove and attended to the vehicle. He kept accounts, logs, and journals; handled the recordings; and labeled the tapes. I mostly just sat and listened and tried to remain patient. From time to time I tried returning to the interview process that had worked originally, but Henry wanted to get Joseph's message on tape—as much as would come. This was definitely Henry speaking or, at best, some fluctuating combination of Henry and Joseph. I kept wanting Henry to stop and let go, to let Joseph come through again as he had once done, but Henry's anxiety and sense of urgency seemed to overshadow Joseph's direct voice. It was all happening more as I had expected than as I had hoped.

There was much that came through in the hours of steady listening and in the midst of all the strange phrases and complicated sentences—much that felt reasonable and relevant—especially as I became increasingly familiar with Henry's style of communication. Had it been otherwise, I should have found myself becoming frustrated in spite of my alleged patience.

Still, it was mostly Henry and not Joseph to whom we lis-

139

tened for all those hours. It was Henry quoting Joseph—generally from memory—from his conversations with Joseph that occurred overnight between our sessions. For the most part, it was barely coherent and a real struggle to listen to hour after hour. The effort was draining both Jerry and me. (Jerry actually became nauseated nearly every day.) It was not because our sessions were complex or esoteric—they were just so redundant and rambling. And there was always so much anxious energy in the room! But sometimes it seemed as though Joseph suddenly began to speak to Henry, and Henry would try to listen and repeat simultaneously. At those times, Henry would quickly put out his cigarette, even if he had just started it. I came to view Henry's smoking behavior as an indication of what was happening between him and Joseph. Whenever Henry would relax a bit, lean back, and light up a cigarette, as though he were taking a break of sorts, Joseph would begin to be heard inside Henry's head. Henry would put out his cigarette, sit up straight, and try hard—too hard, perhaps—to let Joseph come through. It never worked quite the way I had seen it happen that previous time at Henry's house. It never seemed to go quite to Henry's satisfaction. Yet, I continued to feel certain that somewhere in all these words was something very pertinent.

"I keep gettin' in the way," Henry would say. "I don't have too good of words enough to handle it. Besides, I don't have these teeth right up here in front, so I think it's comin' out pretty rough in the pro-nounciation. But he says it's my own mind. It's pretty hard for a human not to get their own mind in the way. It's my outer mind problem, because I can't put that aside."

It would be good, I thought to myself, if Henry could somehow move aside enough at will to let Joseph speak directly or else just be himself and not try to speak for Joseph.

"But Joseph says that this is all okay for him because he wants me here all the time. I'm not to go under any kind of trance or hypnotic effects or any such a kind of concerns. Any kind of such affectations is coming into the problem of

140

loose spirits and imitations. Then this is going to get into the medium problem."

"The medium problem?" I questioned.

"See, this is the reason they don't want to use any trance operations or hypnotics or use any mediumship to come through, because that's used by loose spirits and not used by creation system or spiritual counseling system. Any medium can get any voice or imitation from any kinds of sources. The listening post is going to be in trance, and they don't know nothing. So loose spirits can tell you anything, whatever they want, right or wrong or mixed up both. You never know. People can go to the temptation to get anything from the spirit world, which is not human's business. Loose spirits means having no sense of purpose and service agreements and not open to the most inner masterful part behind the human. They have only relation to outer mind of human, maybe dead human, trying to hide in somebody's body. That's the reason they don't like to use unconscious conditions. Joseph wants you to know that this project is not mediumship action and nobody needs to use outside medium."

Henry now appeared to be free, at least for the moment, from his anxious expounding. He was simply talking, and it was considerably clearer. In his travels, Henry explained, in his search for his "listening post," someone had called him a medium. "The first time I ever heard that word," he said, "I had to ask Joseph, because I didn't know the meaning. I thought it meant open the door to the seventh- and eighth-sense levels to the inner mind, but Joseph says no. Joseph says medium means open to outside influence which is concerned about other people's affairs. So we have to make it clear difference, big difference between inner mind and loose spirit. Lot of these people, they go into trance, they give predictions and tell fortunes, they talk about somebody's personal temptations about money and all such concerns, which is against the law of the spiritual system. Only loose spirits gonna talk about such a concerns. Sometimes it gets pretty close to the truth about what's going to happen and then, oh boy, they give him big credit."

141

"I can understand the danger in using psychics or fortune-tellers in personal or monetary matters, but in what sense is it against the law?"

"That's our own interpretation for our own understanding. That's what Joseph called injustice, because it's going around the other way through the field of injustice. It is backwards because it is mixed up with all those human conditioning. All the selfish concerns for getting this and that is coming out of fear. The creation system doesn't relation to such a concerns because it's only production to even more fear."

He paused, waiting for a comment or a question from me. This was one of the few times that our session even resembled conversation. Most of our sessions required us to sit quietly while Henry went on for hours, filling tape after tape. It occurred to me to ask what Joseph wanted of me—what he intended should come of all these hours of recording. Perhaps a simple question would elicit a brief response. "So where do we go from here?" I asked.

"Well," said Henry, "on your vacation. Where do you go on your vacation?"

We had planned to break for the holidays—from Christmas through New Year's Day—but we had not called it a vacation. Officially, our trip to the West Coast would be part of the project—our chance to contact persons who might be of help to Henry's or Joseph's objectives or to our own understanding. I told him we planned to be in the San Francisco Bay Area, with which he was familiar, and a few other places in California and Oregon.

"I usually head out toward the Mission District," he said. "Way out to Figueroa and Fourteenth and all those places, then way up to Nobb Hill and Golden Gate and all that area. And Joseph goes through when I'm clicking my tongue. Someday I'll show you around."

"Well, that might be good," I allowed, "someday if we get the chance—"

"And what kind of relationship, or I mean, what was your findings with other medicine men? See, I'm not a medicine man."

142

"Yes, I know."

"Gee, there's a lot of things we can do. There's a lot of things we all have to do to get this society back in a little peaceful state and happy state again. This goes first to transportation and then getting into teleportation and levitation and all such pronouncements. This is needed to use for our energy forces procurements. It is the most important request that a human can make to the spirit announcements though themselves."

Teleportation, levitation, energy forces—here and there in Henry's lengthy ramblings, these words had appeared—but almost out of context and without any explanation. "Is this Joseph's message," I asked, "or his purpose—to give information about levitation and teleportation?"

"No!" was the answer. "That comes after. And that's just natural. Coming naturally. It doesn't need any message. The message is only that you are not supposed to violate your neighbor in any form. Then give—giving. And forgiving is right behind that. We are to teach our children the true standard of these golden rules of life, and as to their meaning and as to their use. Then they can bring out their own power inside of them to help with the society's work for the whole of society."

It might be interesting, someday, to be "shown around" San Francisco by Henry and Joseph—that is, if Henry were not invisible and clicking his tongue—I thought to myself as Jerry and I headed west toward San Francisco. But for now I was glad to be getting away. We needed this break from all the talking, and from Henry's intense sense of urgency. In a couple of weeks, I would be back in my chair at Henry's side, watching, listening, hoping to decipher—or develop—the direction and relevance of all these hours of dissertation.

Our time with Henry was more than half over. Yet, I was still not sure at this point whether I was seeking some specific information, preparing to relay a message, serving Joseph, or simply being accommodating to an anxious and dedicated old man. I was willing to return to sit through more lengthy sessions. I would at least finish out the project as we had scheduled it, even though I was not sure now what it would all add up to—or what was to be done with it. I would have the recordings and a chance to listen to all these words again. The problem, it seemed, was how to separate Henry's interference from Joseph's communications. At any rate, there was something meaningful in the arrangement. Just that this sort of phenomenon could happen was important in itself. That this old man—not illiterate but quite un-learned, a member of an almost disregarded minority—could access a variety of ancient and universal philosophies and esoteric concepts, successfully treat himself for alcohol-ism, make dramatic changes in his health and stamina through a sophisticated dietary regimen, and speak know-ingly of contemporary social circumstances and planetary issues—and all entirely from within himself—was not only curious but also significant.

Henry was obviously not a medium or a channel of any sort. He was getting everything he said from his own mind. At times I had wondered why—if there were a Joseph and if there were an urgent message that I was supposed to relay —why Joseph didn't select someone sufficiently articulate and credible. But I had to remind myself that Joseph was an aspect of Henry or, actually, the other way around. Henry was repeating, or trying to repeat as best he could, what he was in the process of learning from his own self.

I had seen Henry's health improve even during the brief time that I was with him. Before we met him, he told us, he could not lift his arms as high as his head. His people told us the same thing. In fact, they claimed he had made an almost total character change. "Like a new person," they said. In past years, he had spent a lot of time in hospitals, but no doctor, according to him, ever spoke with him about his health. He told us once that doctors at the Indian hospital used to "fool around" with him, as he put it, sending him up and down the halls for tests and samples and even opera-tions. "But they never explained or asked anything," he said. "You'd think just once someone would have asked me what

I was eating and how I was living. Joseph is the ony one who ever talked to me about my health and my diet." So Joseph, whoever he was, was actually giving him concrete advice and education. There was no external source or influence to account for Henry's new education. Joseph was training Henry.

I was looking forward to discussing Henry and Joseph with Jack Schwarz, and after our Christmas holiday in San Francisco, we headed up to Jack's place in Grant's Pass, Oregon. Though I had known Jack and Lois for many years, I had never been to their home. We had been invited to their traditional New Year's Eve party in Grant's Pass, and I could only hope that I would have some opportunity before, during, or after the party for a few private moments with Jack.

Some years before, Jack had been involved with the Voluntary Controls Program at The Menninger Foundation, where he had demonstrated his ability to control psychophysiological states and processes normally considered involuntary. Some of these demonstrations had been documented in the Hartley Productions film *Biofeedback: The Yoga of the West,* and partly owing to this film, Jack had become known for his unusual abilities. His abilities to control bleeding and pain and other "involuntary" processes were evident not only on the film but also on the polygraph records produced in the laboratory. Through his books and lectures and his training programs at his Aletheia Foundation, he was also known for his teachings on health, healing, and human potential. I had occasionally sought his advice on a number of issues regarding myself and my work, and I had become well aware and appreciative of his intuitive abilities.

I felt that Jack's intuitive insight could offer some useful information about this Henry-Joseph phenomenon and its significance. Jack had never seen or heard about Henry, but I had with me a couple of photographs of him. Jack could see auras. He could read people's moods and personality characteristics and could see their capacities and potentials as well as diseases and nutritional deficiencies—just by

145

looking. I had found that he could also see these things by "reading" a photograph; it was part of his "normal" vision. Whatever it was that Jack saw, I knew he referred to it, or at least part of it, as "almost physical," and he considered this ability to be part of the human potential.

When we arrived at the party, we found an abundance of food and games. Jerry actually won a little token trophy in a game of darts. Then there was a demonstration of sorts— "just for laughs," as Jack put it. It was a sort of tongue-in-cheek psychic demonstration in which Jack was to identify an object in the room to be chosen in his absence. The game plan was that someone would hold Jack's hand and follow along behind with eyes closed, allowing Jack to lead the way while the person would actually be leading Jack "psychically" by holding a mental picture of the preselected object. Jerry was the "imager" who held Jack's hand; and the game was successful, or at least interesting, because after a couple of circles around the room, Jack went directly to the chosen little doll, which stood among others on a shelf in the corner. Jerry was the only one who had not known Jack for some time, and I wondered whether Jack had somehow sensed his curiosity and conducted that little game for his benefit.

Jack had also sensed the photographs that I was carrying with me, I discovered, and I was glad I had not hastily brought them out at the first opportunity. I had with me my pictures of Henry and also a portrait of an acquaintance who was attempting to overcome a rather serious illness. Soon after midnight, most of the guests began to leave, and Jack found a quiet moment to spend with Jerry and me. He offered a sort of reading for Jerry that was very brief but very positive and complimentary.

"I just wanted to share that, since you two are working together," Jack said. "You know I usually avoid this at these social events. You can't believe the things people asked of me—right here at the party. Maybe you didn't notice. That's why I really appreciate that you didn't ask me to look at the pictures."

So I simply waited until after we had left and later sent a picture of Henry to Jack in an envelope without a request or

146

a word of explanation. I did not see Jack again until months later—until after we had completed the recording project with Henry and Joseph. Jack I were both speakers at a seminar in Kansas, and I had the opportunity to hear what he had to say. Jack volunteered his comments without my even needing to bring the matter up. By now I had already learned much of what he was able to tell me, but his comments did provide some further understanding, and a useful confirmation of Henry's explanation of how his "opening" to his "inner mind" had come about. Jack did not have the photograph with him at the time, but apparently he had studied it, and he spoke from memory as though he were seeing it at the moment. I had told Jack nothing about Henry. I had not even explained why I had sent him the photograph.

"There's a real problem with the liver," he said. "There is still considerable toxicity which should be taken care of."

"Well, that's because he used to be an alcoholic," I explained, "but he claims that's been taken care of."

"I know. And I know it's improved. But there is still something that can be done. The man is elderly, and he's not as strong as he wants to be. There are some treatments that might be helpful."

"Henry's had a lot of problems with his health," I said, "but he is improving steadily. I think he's changed considerably just in the time I've known him. Anyway, this isn't exactly the issue that—"

"I know," Jack repeated. "You want to talk about the guidance from his inner self. What you're wanting to know about is what has happened with Henry. This is what we call being born again—in the real meaning of the term. If you will check with his recent history, you will find he had a catastrophic episode a number of years ago—like an accident or injury—somewhere around late 1972 or early 1973—in which he experienced a death or near-death."

"He got struck by a car and was seriously injured. And he speaks of it as part of Joseph's arrangement for him."

"This is where it begins. This is the arrangement that you are seeing in him—"

"He calls himself a mutant," I interjected.

147

"Well, whatever he calls it. This episode symbolizes the end of his life. At that time Henry had finished with his own personal agenda, and since Henry's life was actually over, it was available to the inner being who chose to use this life for his own agenda—which is different from Henry's. This is theoretically a possibility that could happen to anyone. But generally human beings are occupied with their own karma until they die."

"Henry refers to this inner being as Joseph. But he says that this is just a way of providing some reference for himself, since the inner mind appears to be a separate being."

"Exactly. And this is the real meaning of what we call being born again. You have no doubt heard the term in a different sense, because it is misused."

"What is the purpose of this sort of thing happening to a person like Henry?"

"Well, the purpose is Joseph's. If there had been no purpose, of course, it wouldn't have happened. Such a thing must be arranged."

"Henry has explained it that way, I guess. I mean the arrangement, anyway. Henry says Joseph had to open the door from the other side."

"That's right. It's arranged on the other side."

After two weeks on the West Coast, we headed back to Idaho to continue our regular recording sessions. They were much the same as they had been before, which was somewhat discouraging, because our time with Henry was nearly over, at least for this phase of the project. Again, in our continuing sessions, Henry used words such as antigravity, levitation, telepathy, and reincarnation. He spoke of the pyramids in Egypt, of pyramids in general, and made references to the Aztecs and the Incas. Though I was recording all his words, I made note of these references, because often they were thrown out as an aside and without detail or were used in a context that seemed unrelated or unclear, and I thought they might be key references, worth pursuing later. I was not sure whether I would be coming back again to spend more time with Henry—even if he should wish it. But I did expect that I would be able to assist by making contacts for him.

Then one day Henry announced that Joseph might soon be inviting me to question him directly. "Joseph says that you have given a lot of time recording what we have to say and we should give you some chance to ask a few questions before you leave. Then the next steps we have to find after that. I have done my best as much as I could. Just like I told you, it's pretty hard not to get my own mind in the way. Sometimes Joseph can talk directly. Sometimes I'm listening and I'm talking at the same time."

A few days later, Henry told me the time had come and Joseph was ready for my questions. "Now today, Joseph says you just go ahead and ask anything you want, and I don't have to worry about it. Whatever topic you want, and just let Joseph refer to your concerns."

I began to consider what to ask. I could not know how many questions I might be allowed or how Henry might deal with them. I wanted to be very direct and to avoid, if possible, invoking the same lengthy and somewhat rambling expoundings that we had already recorded.

Henry interrupted my thoughts. "Now first, before you get started with it, I wanted to tell you a little story for just a minute. Joseph says, 'Okay, Henry, you go ahead,' because I forgot to tell you before. And this happened when I was a pretty young kid in the Indian school. We were supposed to have sharing in our class from time to time—you know sharing?—to tell about whatever we wanted to share with our classmates. Well, one kid, he never got up, so the teacher made him get up. Well, he just stood there. He didn't know what to say, so the teacher told him to say something about whatever he might have seen on his way to school this morning. So he began thinkin' about it and finally he says, 'Well, I saw a boid in a tree.' The teacher says, 'Now you don't call that a boid, you know better than that. That was no boid in that tree.' And this young kid, he says, 'Well, then, I don't know. He sure choiped like a boid.' "

Jerry and I laughed, but Henry, who was frequently smiling and chuckling, remained serious. "Joseph says we better go ahead now. I just been wanting to tell you that because that's your name, as you know, so I thought you might be interested. But Joseph says you just go ahead now and ask your questions."

Then Henry appeared to simply let go. He sat there quietly with a comfortable expression on his face. I had never seen him this way. Either he was relaxing with his cigarette and his small talk, or he was really working at talking for Joseph, trying to concentrate and often looking strained. Now he looked ready and waiting—and completely receptive.

I had not prepared any questions, but I thought immediately of some of the expressions and remarks that I had noted over the past days. I would ask regarding these. "Joseph!" I said in a determined voice, trying to sound confident that I was addressing him directly. "There have been several mentions here of pyramids. These days we hear various new ideas about pyramids—about the ancient ones and how they were constructed, and about various new uses for pyramids. Can you tell me something precise about them? What exactly is their significance?"

"There are various uses, but no new uses. There is nothing newly discovered or newly mentioned about pryamids. In the future, as in the past, they will be used for their mummifying capacity. The pyramid is the best geometric form available as a physical structure to use for the preservation of perishables."

For the first time in all these days that we had been driving from Boise to Nampa, I believed I was really hearing Joseph, just as I had that day at Henry's house when Joseph spoke of human "defects" and asked me to remain patient with Henry. But now I tried not to look surprised or even to give it much thought. I did not want to do anything to interfere, and Joseph was continuing.

"The original use of the ancient pyramids on this planet was something else. They were built to be communication devices and not tombs. They worked like aiming antennae for projecting and receiving vibrations. They were for communication among planets and various dimensions. They do not serve in that way now, and for that reason they should all be defused."

He paused, perhaps to wait for my next question, but I wanted him to go on without stopping. I did not want this circumstance to change.

"Defused?" I asked quickly.

"Most of them are defused. Those with flat tops are defused. Now all the tops should be removed, and therefore the crystals which they contain. So the pyramids do not have their original significance. It might be good if you understand that they were put together by using the art of moving heavy objects free of the force of attraction, which here would be named gravity. It is already quite late for modern humans to understand this, but this knowledge is held back because of humans' fear of one another. Levitation was known to ancient cultures, but where evidence exists, you try to explain it in other ways. The knowledge is required for survival because it is the only answer to the energy crisis which would destroy humanity. So you might consider that the significance of the pyramids is a hint that objects can be moved and transported by what we have called levitation. Huge stones can be floated in the air as in a vacuum."

"I wanted to ask about levitation. You—or Henry—mentioned levitation several times, and also teleportation. Is it important to understand? And, if so, how do we explain how it is done?"

"The knowledge is necessary and you are suffering without it, but there is no explanation. It comes like any other ability, like moving your lungs or your legs or picking up something. It is the natural use of your human energy—it is nothing like strain or compression—not like the wasteful and dangerous process of exploding petroleum."

"You mentioned a vacuum. Henry once said something about creating a vacuum around an object. Is this what you mean? How is such a vacuum created?"

"It is sound, pure sound—not that you can hear—sound

151

beyond hearing. So you cannot observe it, though you can observe the result. It needs no explanation. You have another question."

I was amazed at what was happening. This was definitely Henry's own voice, but it was far from Henry's manner of speaking. This was the most direct and clear communication I had received, and it was my opportunity to at least make clear for myself a number of important but foggy references. "I wanted to ask you about reincarnation. Henry has mentioned reincarnation, also, on several occasions, but has only used the word as his explanation for changing the subject or leaving something out. He mentions it as though he doesn't want to talk about it. He is saying, or you have said, that this is none of the people's business—that's the way it was put."

"How can Henry talk about reincarnation?"

There was a long pause.

"Why not?" I asked.

"The question is how. How will he speak of it? Will he say that he will reincarnate one day? This would be inaccurate. When Henry is gone, he is gone. Henry is a temporary manifestation, and there will never be another Henry. Once Henry understands this, Henry cannot speak of his own reincarnation. Next he will want to say that since he is temporary and I, Joseph, am eternal, then it must be Joseph who reincarnates. But I am intangible and always have been. Henry cannot reincarnate, and I will never be incarnate. What is there to reincarnate?"

"So, are you saying there is no reincarnation?"

"No. I can speak of reincarnation, because I am not human. The humans, as humans, want to say, 'I was this or that, and I will be this or that.' It may confuse who is who. Some humans may benefit by contemplating reincarnation. It depends on who they are. But it can at times be distracting to the immediate work of the temporary instrument—especially at this time."

"Is that the sense in which you say that it is none of the humans' business? And why especially at this time?"

152

"In the sense that it is a distraction. The humans can find so many distractions. At this time there's the problem of the humans' trying to amuse themselves by concerning themselves with our business. They distract themselves from their own work. They may know about us—the spiritual counseling system—and that we are available to them. But it is dangerous for the humans to think that their duty to the Earth can be avoided by pretending to have some important career in the spirit world. It's like a new fashion for people to preach that if enough humans would just concentrate on how wonderful is the heaven up in the sky, the problems on the Earth will disappear. They think they could get peace from heaven without efforts. Well, that's not what humans are created for. The spirit world takes good care of its affairs. What remains is for the humans to get to work with their own business."

"What is the humans' business?" I asked.

"The petroleum problem!" The response came swift and loud, and then there was a pause, as though to allow for my complete comprehension.

The petroleum problem, I thought to myself. It was an encompassing example. It related not only to the contemporary energy crisis, which was a major planetary issue, but also to the energy alternative potentials which Joseph had said were required for the future. The petroleum problem, as Joseph had called it, played a central role in economic problems everywhere and in the world as a whole, and was also a major factor in the pollution of the human environment as well as the destruction of the natural world..

"Saving the world," Joseph went on, now speaking slowly and quietly. "Simply the humans saving themselves. They don't need to worry about us. We will take care of our own affairs. The humans' business is to get to work with their physical equipment and take care of their planet. That's the humans' business—to pay attention to energy and education and their environment, to look after each other and life on the Earth. This is the reason for their physical existence as instruments."

Joseph stopped. Unless I had another question, he had

said all he would say. I sat quietly, still thinking about "the petroleum problem" and "the humans' business." I felt there was some further explanation—some question that still remained—and I wanted to get a grasp on it while Joseph was available. It seemed that the energy problem, which had many times been mentioned during our recording sessions, necessitated, or at least justified, pursuing the alternatives of which Joseph had spoken. Levitation? Teleportation? But Joseph said there is no explaining. Then the task is something other than to learn about these things.

"Joseph, you speak of humans saving themselves. Without the explanations, where do we begin? How are humans qualified—or capable of taking care of the planet?"

"The four laws. The four laws have been given. You have already recorded the four laws: Love your God, love your neighbor, give, and forgive. The problems are based on fear. People want this and that, to get so many things, more than they need. You call it greed, but it's based on fear. It grows steadily worse because others don't have their basic needs, and this makes your world unsafe. If people can be free of this fear, they can take care of each other. So these four laws are related. Love your neighbor means do not violate your fellow human being in any way. Love your God means see your God as your own self within you. Don't think that God is outside of you—up in the sky somewhere, frowning at you. If you think God is looking down from above, pointing a finger in judgment and anger, you cannot love your neighbor. You cannot be giving, and you will not believe in forgiving. Forgiving means you don't violate in return one who has violated you. No God would do that. Never, never desire revenge. So this is the people's business."

"And this in itself will take care of the whole economy," I remarked. It sounded sarcastic. I had not meant it that way. I had not even intended to say it.

"Because it directs action. It gets to the reverse side of greed and temptation and allows all those natural abilities you were thinking about. The whole economy? What is that? It's a joint account. One joint account belongs to each and every one on the face of this Earth."

154

There was another pause, and I had no further questions. I felt complete and satisfied. Yet, I wondered whether something further was expected of this project. I wondered whether I had some responsibility, now, while I had the chance, to get some detailed specifics on such attractive subjects as levitation, teleportation, and interplanetary communication.

But Henry lit a cigarette. He looked comfortable and pleased and not at all exhausted. He seemed, in fact, quite energized and went on talking cheerfully until well after dark —about his health, his childhood, and his wonderful skill at making sourdough bread. Finally, we were able to get away for the drive back to Boise.

On the day of our departure, I assured him I would one day be in touch, and I would do my best to arrange some useful introductions for him. He seemed sorry to see us leave and began to appear somewhat anxious and apprehensive again, but he had a big smile as he stood out in the snow in front of the trailer, waving until we were out of sight.

◑   ◑   ◑

About a year after our project in Idaho, I invited Henry to a meeting near Kansas City, Missouri, sponsored by the Cross-Cultural Studies Program, in which we brought together traditional spokespersons and representatives from a variety of cultures along with a number of researchers and educators. This gathering was not related to the Henry-Joseph project, for Henry's work and focus was something other than as a cultural representative, but I wanted to provide some additional contacts for Henry and to allow others a chance to see and hear from him. My own direct involvement with Henry was thus completed, except perhaps to facilitate further contacts as requested, and after our meeting in Missouri, I did not see him again.

The Henry-Joseph experience had not been a research project in the usual sense. There was no specific new data to report. There was no scientific investigation or finding. There was no new metaphysical or esoteric revelation. What there was was the story itself. I said as much one day to

155

someone who had been involved in supporting our project. I said that what had interested me about this project was the phenomenon itself.

"Phenomena aren't important," came the response. "They might be fascinating or far out, but they don't mean much in themselves."

I agreed, and so I wondered if perhaps I had chosen the wrong word. Phenomenon? I had intended it to mean that the arrangement itself was meaningful—the appearance of a very real and powerful inner wisdom in a man such as Henry. What I had heard from Joseph was important because it was a confirmation of the reality that is behind our very existence. It was in itself a message of encouragement and empowerment. Had I been searching for treasures from the realm of the occult, I might as well have gone to the library. No, the project was for the story itself—and such a story serves more than erudition. It evokes a response.

During the time that I was arranging the Henry-Joseph project, I was offered a guided tour through a vast and remarkable Theosophical library in southern California. It was one of the most impressive I had ever seen, containing rare and ancient books as well as contemporary esoteric documents and journals. Two thoughts occurred to me even as I stood among all those volumes. Humans have accumulated in printed form an almost unfathomable amount of knowledge and information on everything from the cellular to the cosmic, from physics to metaphysics, from the scientific to the spiritual. While it may be awesome to consider that we could go on reading and researching to the end of our lives and cover not more than a fraction of all that has been discovered, documented, detailed, and described, it is exciting to expect to go on learning forever. But it also occurred to me that our accumulated and available knowledge is irreconcilable with our circumstances. Our contemporary planetary emergency is not owing to a lack of information. It is not what we do not know but what we do not do that is the problem of our time, though perhaps this was not so in the past.

*All the words and works of all the mystics, magicians, and
medicine people whom we encounter in our own lives is but
a resonance of what has been experienced and expounded
many times throughout the history of our world. It is not that
we might be gifted with some untold revelation that we encounter these people—it is that we might be moved to participate in their stories. Their stories are what matter—the
events of their lives that serve as example and encouragement. We come to know such people not only to repeat what
they said but also to allow their words to move us into action.*

*On the first day of my acquaintance with Swami Rama,
before I had ever been to India, we stood in the library of the
Greens' home in Topeka, Kansas, and he spoke of taking me
to see his country. "Here we will first do our work," he said,
"and then we will go to India. I will take you to see those
saints and sages who live in the caves high in the Himalayas.
And you will have a chance to put your questions."*

*"My questions?" I responded. What questions did he sup-
pose I would ask?*

*"No, no, you must put your questions," he said insistently.
" 'For what do you remain here sitting on the mountain?' you
will ask. 'Are you sick?' You can put such questions directly
to their faces. 'When there is war and hunger and so many
sufferings, why do you go on hiding in a cave? If you are so
enlightened as they say, why do you not come down and do
something useful?' Oh, such a challenge you will put, you
see? But then, they have not to answer, for perhaps you
cannot understand."*

*He stood grinning at me, as though he were attempting to
bewilder me for his own amusement. Then his face became
serious, and he nearly shouted at me: "The leaves would not
grow on the trees nor the rivers flow in their beds were it not
for those saintly masters who attend to their duties here on
Earth! Do you think they merely sit to indulge in blissful
state? Then they could as well simply leave this earthly
plane. Like transmitters and receivers, they assist in looking
after these worldly functions. Every single manifest being
comes forth in order to serve in this world."*

157

The image that his words invoked—as well as his booming voice—made a lasting impact. At times, hearing those words, I thought about myself and all my friends and about what it is, really, that we are all doing here. And, looking back over my many years in the Far East at all the Asian faces I could still clearly recall, I thought about the vast variety of manifest beings who had come forth on both sides of this Earth to share and to serve in our collective planetary affairs.

● ● ●

Planetary affairs. The message is so simple that it is elusive. It is so simple that it is a challenge to understand. "The message," as Henry put it, "is only that you are not supposed to violate your neighbor in any form." The message is "give" and "forgive." It is ironic that the simplest ideas are often the most difficult to work with. The so-called "extraordinary" or "paranormal" feats are easy by comparison.

I can elicit attention by the very mention of levitation and teleportation. "Show me how!" people will say, and they will become filled with desire—willing to pursue and to practice if only they be told the techniques. But "love thy neighbor, give and forgive" sounds more like a prayer than a practice. It may be nice, but it doesn't entice. Peculiar personal powers seem more readily attainable. Suppose we were to establish a great mystery school, open to anyone who wished to attend, and everyone had to choose one of three electives. They could pursue levitation, they could practice teleportation, or they could work on being always loving, always giving and forgiving, never violating anyone. I wonder how the classes would fill? It is a matter of considerable concern. Suppose there were a large number of people who could achieve levitation and teleportation (and who knows what next?) who could not love, give, or forgive.

I asked Henry whether the purpose of Joseph's message was to give information about teleportation and levitation. "No," he said, "that comes after. And that's just natural. Coming naturally. It doesn't need any message." I believe that Joseph's message was about human potential and re-

sponsibility—that they are inseparable. The most purposeful, practical, and powerful of all the great laws of the universe, it seems to me, is the principle of right relations. Herein lies the ultimate human potential. With these "golden rules of life," as Henry put it, we can bring out our own power. It comes naturally.

I realized that Joseph had indeed explained, as succinctly as it can be done, how levitation and other such natural powers are manifested. He had explained so that if anyone should inquire as to the precise technique, the answer is there. The powers are manifested through the transcending of fear. "Don't violate in return one who has violated you. . . . Never, never desire revenge." Fear is the obstacle. Transcending fear, and thus rising above the blinding obstructions that fear puts in the way, is like getting over and beyond a great wall and finding that these special human-potential capacities we had been struggling for are simply waiting there.

"Do not violate your neighbor" does not mean just the folks next door. "Do not violate your neighbor" has become a planetary affair. And we're all involved in planetary affairs now—every one of us. Saving the world—this is the humans' business. "It gets to the reverse side of greed and temptation," Joseph had said, "and allows all those natural abilities you were thinking about." Human potential? Natural powers? They're not a matter of personal acquisition. It's all a matter of love.

◐　　◐　　◐

On a clear, quiet evening one late spring, a few of us sat chatting on the doorstep in front of Rolling Thunder's house. Rolling Thunder and his sons were away, but his wife, Spotted Fawn, was there with us. She sat quietly, watching her kittens frolicking about in the yard, apparently absorbed in her own thoughts. One of them kept scampering up and down the tree trunk behind her in a wild frenzy, and Spotted Fawn plucked it from the tree and placed it gently in her lap. "You're freaking out, Patrol Car," she said, stroking it gently.

159

"Calm down." It seemed to have an immediate effect. This little kitten was the friskiest and fastest of the litter. It was mostly black, but it had white on its sides, and so it had been named Patrol Car.

From somewhere there appeared a tiny baby frog. The nearest stream was a ways away, and this little creature must have hopped a long while to get so far astray from his companions. "Hey, little fellow!" Spotted Fawn exclaimed. "Aren't you a little young to be running away?" Patrol Car crawled down from her lap to have a closer look. "See? He's even smaller than you are," said Spotted Fawn. "Isn't he cute?" Patrol Car made a quick swipe with his paw and flipped the little frog into the air. The frog landed and hopped, and Patrol Car pounced. Spotted Fawn snatched the kitten and held it to her face. "How would you like it if someone did that to you?" She held Patrol Car tightly in her lap and nudged the frog until it started on its way.

I watched her holding her kitten, and in an instant, a number of spontaneous thoughts flashed through my mind. It was as though I became aware of a half-dozen enigmas simultaneously without a moment to think them through: Can a kitten be expected to repress its natural instincts? Shouldn't nature be left alone to take its own course? Don't things happen as they are meant to? Was this not intervention? Wherein lies our right to interfere with the flow of fate? Are we always to think ourselves responsible?

Spotted Fawn looked at me as though she were aware of my thoughts and said quietly, "When we're here, we're part of the picture."

SCENE EIGHT

The Story Continues

One day while I was living in the San Francisco Bay Area, I went back to Rolling Thunder's house in Carlin, Nevada, for a visit. Nearly a year had passed since I and my Japanese friend Tsutomu had made the trip by train to close out my Carlin apartment. Since then I had not been back, though I had met with Rolling Thunder a couple of times in San Francisco. With his job on the railroad, his visits to the reservations, his work on human rights and land issues, and his responsibilities as a spokesman and medicine man, Rolling Thunder's life remained involved and eventful.

I took a Greyhound bus east on Highway 80 to Carlin and checked into the State Inn just as I had done when I had first arrived in Carlin to look up Rolling Thunder. The same elderly woman was still there, shuffling along in her slippers. A single room was still the same low price.

"I've been here before," I said. "That was nearly three years ago, and I stayed here several days."

She looked up at me and squinted through her glasses. "Oh yeah? Well, lots of people has."

When I got to Rolling Thunder's place, I was surprised to

be greeted at the door by Inga, the young woman from Denmark, who had traveled with us to witness and photograph the destruction of the pinyon forests on Indian land. She had since gone home to Denmark but had recently come again to the United States. Rolling Thunder was still working for the railroad, and he was out on a trip—just as I had expected.

"Come on in," she said. "Come on in and sit down. Where are all your things?"

"I'm staying in the motel up on the highway."

"Why?"

"Well, I wasn't sure who would be here or how long I'd be around."

"Spotted Fawn's in Elko. She'll be back pretty soon."

As we sat and talked, I heard the native sounds of Indian chanting. As soon as I became aware of the singing, I thought of David Monongye, the well-known Hopi elder, and I wondered why. She and I sat and chatted for a long time. We talked about Denmark and her family and about the time when Rolling Thunder went to Stockholm to attend the International Conference on the Human Environment. We talked about recent people and events at Rolling Thunder's place.

But most of my mind remained attentive to the singing in the other room, and I kept seeing images of Grandfather David. Somehow it felt to me as though it were David's voice coming through that door. Yet I knew it could not be David. This was not even Hopi singing. She noticed me staring at the open bedroom door.

"Oh, by the way, David Monongye is here. He's in that room."

"You mean that really is David?"

"Yes. Well, what? You mean the music? Of course not. David's nearly dead. We're playing records for him. Rolling Thunder wants us to keep the music going all the time."

David Monongye, I learned, had recently been brought here and left in Rolling Thunder's hands by his friends, and he was on the threshold of death. His friends had not wanted him to travel because they had feared he could not make the journey. But David had insisted. The only words he had been able to say were: "Take me to Rolling Thunder. Take me to Rolling Thunder." So David had been delivered, and he had been given a room and a bed so he could rest and drink a special herbal tea until he became strong enough and conscious enough to receive Rolling Thunder's healing ritual.

That evening when Spotted Fawn returned from Elko, she went in and out of David's room many times, either to change the music or to take him more tea or simply to speak to him some words of reassurance and comfort.

It was late when I returned to my room in the motel up on the highway. Walking back across the railroad tracks and through the town of Carlin, I easily remembered the days and the events when I and several colleagues and members of the Committee of Concern for the Traditional Indian were living here and working with Rolling Thunder. But once back in my motel room, I lay awake in the darkness and thought about David Monongye. Perhaps he was dying indeed. No one knew his age for certain. The records from the previous century were insufficient. But he had been a schoolboy in the days of the great conflicts when all the native peoples were known as hostiles. By matching his schoolday memories with various historic events, his people calculated his age to be well over one hundred.

Though I had not seen him for some months, I could recall him clearly in my mind. I could hear his strong, determined voice and picture his silver-grey hair and crimson scarf headband. I could picture that small face and those huge, thick glasses through which he had not seen a thing for several years.

The last time I had been with Grandfather David, I was staying in Berkeley with Rolling Thunder. Rolling Thunder had been involved in a complicated struggle, and he was in retreat in my friend's home in the Berkeley Hills. David had come to the Bay Area to speak at the Ecology Center in San Francisco, and members of the Committee of Concern had brought him to Berkeley to meet with Rolling Thunder before his return to Arizona. That night, we had all gone with Rolling

Thunder to the top of the Berkeley Hills far above the University of California campus. This was to be the last of several peyote tea ceremonies on this hilltop, and now that Grandfather David would be with us, Rolling Thunder wanted it to be a special prayer offering for him.

Rolling Thunder and his family, David Monongye, several of the Committee members, and I crowded into three cars and made our way through the darkness up the bumpy, winding dirt roads to the top of the hill. We built the sacred fire with kindling, sticks, and logs that we had carried from the woodshed at the house, and Spotted Fawn carefully placed on the edge of the fire the pot of tea that she had steeped at the house before we left. As the medicine tea reheated, we gathered around the fire, making a tight circle. We stared down into the darting flames.

Old Grandfather David, wrapped in an old blanket, was helped from the car and led to the fireside. In his cupped hands before him he held his ever-present cornmeal in readiness for his offering and his prayer. Morning Star removed the cups from the box and placed them carefully on the ground, close to the steaming teapot, and one of Rolling Thunder's sons fetched his medicine bag from the car.

When the tea was poured into the cups and distributed around the fire, Rolling Thunder announced that David had been undergoing a different medicine treatment and that it would therefore not be appropriate for him to partake of the peyote tea. "But now at this time," he said, "David will offer the first prayer."

David stepped cautiously toward the fire, feeling his way with the toes of his shoes, and when he was standing directly over the flames and the smoke was rising right into his face, he began to speak softly. I could not understand his Hopi language, but I supposed that he was speaking about health —health for himself, health for all of us on this hilltop, health for his people, and health for the Earth. This was the way American Indians always spoke, as far as I knew. To them it was all the same health—from the person to the environment to the planet. There was only one health.

164

Leaning over the fire, David completed his soft-spoken invocation and slowly sprinkled the cornmeal into the flickering fire. We stood for a long while in silence. It was inspiring to watch this old man as he made his offering. I knew that in his one hundred or more years on this Earth he had done this thing a thousand times.

When David had returned to his place in the circle, Rolling Thunder stepped forward to offer his sacrifice to the fire and to say his invocation. He stooped briefly to put something into the flames and then stood tall and looked into the sky. I assumed he was speaking in English, but I could only guess at his words—he was speaking too softly for any of us to hear more than a mumble. This was unusual for him. Usually he spoke, at least in part, for the benefit of all who were present at the ceremony. Now he went on for a long time as we stood silently in our circle. I knew he was not praying solely for his own benefit; but whatever he was saying—and for whomever or whatever—it apparently did not require that we hear and understand the words. Silently, I said my own prayer to myself. I supposed Grandfather David had prayed for the planet, and I wanted to add my own invocation in support of his.

Somewhere in my recollection of my own invocation, I fell asleep. But I must have gone on dreaming in the Berkeley Hills. When I awoke in my room at the State Inn, it seemed for a fleeting second that I had fallen asleep during the ceremony. Then I remembered I was in Carlin, and I spent a few moments recalling my first stay in this motel—the time I ventured out to contact Rolling Thunder, not even knowing for sure whether I could find him or what might happen if I did. My thoughts suddenly turned to Grandfather David, lying ill at Rolling Thunder's, and I got up and went back to the house.

Rolling Thunder had just arrived home from a trip, and he talked to me about Grandfather David. "He was in no shape to travel when they brought him here. In fact, he was almost

165

dead. But he insisted on coming. He's improving, though, and he's gettin' a little bit better. He's taking some special herbs, and that's helping. The main thing, he's got to have attention. We've got several of the women here looking after him all the time. They kind of rotate with it. No more than a few minutes pass that he's left alone. They don't stay in there. He's got to have his rest. He just needs to know he's being looked after, so they go in and out all the time. They keep a record playing, so they've got to keep goin' in to change the record and give him his tea. And I've got a little bell rigged up for him above his bed with a string he can pull if he needs anything. Well, he pulls it all the time, even when they keep goin' in there anyway. Attention. That's the most important thing. We'll have a healing ceremony for him one of these nights when he's well enough to take it. I'll have to do it right out back here. He won't be strong enough to be taken far away."

I recalled that Rolling Thunder once explained why he avoided performing healing rituals at his home. Several rituals had taken place out in the hills when I was living there, near where we had been camping in the canyon. But they had happened in the wide-open spaces, far from anyone's home. To administer herbs and such is one thing, he had told me, but to dislodge live negative forces around a dwelling can put all the inhabitants at risk. Such negative energies and entities can easily make a home of a room, a closet, or even a sofa; they become entrenched and difficult to disperse.

Old David did indeed improve, and on the third day that I was there, as I was sitting in the living room, I heard David talking, weakly but cheerfully, every time someone went into his room. "Go on in there and talk to him," Rolling Thunder urged me. "He knows you, doesn't he? You should go in and talk to him and let him talk to you. That's what he needs." I looked in through the open door. "Go ahead. Go ahead on in. You have to talk loud, you know, or he won't hear you. And he's blind and can't see you. But then, yet, he can see you at that—in his own way, you know."

I went up to the side of the bed. David stared into space just above my head. "You used to meet me out in San Francisco? Yeah, well, I might remember that—that's nice that you did that. I'd like to go out to San Francisco and talk to the people. Maybe you could help me? When I get up and about, well, maybe we could go on out there together."

I was not sure what I ought to say. "I remember the first time I heard you speak out there. That was in the ecology center."

"Oh yeah. Well—uh—ecology—now that's something there. Some changes are taking place and uh—" He paused and breathed deeply. I wondered if he'd lost his train of thought. "Well, we're actually looking forward to some coming changes, to some things—to—uh—what's going to happen. Some things we are supposed to do—well, we've been informed about that. We have to—I don't know why we don't hurry up, some things we're supposed to do right now. That's why we went out and talked to the people. I talked for a long many years, but nobody did much yet. I got pretty tuckered out. Now I have to try to get up and speak again—all over again."

It was sad to hear him talk this way, and I thought perhaps I was tiring him, not helping him. I had not intended this sort of conversation. Yet, he looked stimulated and not at all uncomfortable.

"Well, we know the prophecy and we know it's gonna be good. Changes are coming and it's going to scare the people. But the people brought it on. So it has to readjust. Everything just goes back to good again. Just like me, I came up here to get well again. The life is going to return back to the good way—the sacred way—that's what we're lookin' forward to. Yeah, well, I'd sure like to go around and talk to the people."

He knew when I had left the room—he knew he was alone again—and yet he went on talking aloud. It was a good sign. His voice was getting stronger. I could hear him from the living room: "Come to get well again. Get up and go around again. Talk to the people. Return back to the good way.

We're gonna make a good life for one another—brothers and sisters." For a moment I thought one of us ought to go back in there. It felt strange to leave him talking to himself. But then he switched to Hopi. He wasn't talking to us. He wasn't talking to himself. Let it happen, I thought, even if he is over one hundred. Let him live to see his prayer come true.

●   ●   ●

On the night of the healing ceremony, David called us all into his room, and there were more than a half-dozen of us sitting cross-legged on the floor by his bed. David was helped to sit on the floor in front of us and managed, with the support of the bed against his back, to sit up straight. His hair was combed. He wore his headband and his thick glasses, and he looked dignified. He began to speak in English and then fell into Hopi. But after only a moment, he stopped and stretched a trembling arm toward the corner of the room.

"Well—uh—would you hand me—uh—hand me the little sack there in my baggage. Could you get it?" He waved his outstretched hand, feeling the air. "Should be right there. Right up in top there? A little sack."

Someone found the paper bag and got it into his hands. David felt his way inside the sack and took out a pinch of cornmeal and placed it into his palm.

"Okay, now—uh—now I'm gonna give a prayer. Well, this little prayer for everybody here." Again he spoke a few words in Hopi. "Well—uh—I asked for peace for everybody and—uh—so they may be taken care of and protected through the difficulties that might lie ahead of us, and on the other side of this we could achieve . . . well, that we come to understand one another and respect one another. And—uh—that's what I have said, and I have prayed in that way."

Rolling Thunder asked us to leave him alone with David, and we waited in the living room. Hours later, when the ceremonial fire was made ready in back of the house, we all filed out through the kitchen. David was helped to his feet and out the door and into an old wooden chair that had been placed by the fire. His wrinkled hands were still tightly squeezing his sacred cornmeal.

As always, Rolling Thunder's pipe was lit and the opening invocation was made. A small portion of David's cornmeal was distributed to each of us who stood around the fire. In turn, we spoke our brief words for David and for whatever else we wished to pray might come to pass, and stepping forward, we dusted the cornmeal from our palms into the fire.

Rolling Thunder worked especially long and hard at this healing, but his method and all the steps of the ritual were the same as they had been since I had first witnessed his healings. Perhaps the only difference was that Rolling Thunder did not this time seek any words of invocation or commitment from his patient. David had said his prayer inside. His prayer had been made a thousand times.

Again, as always, Rolling Thunder changed. If his body was not transformed, it seemed so. His manner and his movements were changed. Perhaps it was the semidarkness or the flickering firelight, but if I squinted, I could see, or at least feel, the animals that I had sometimes sensed before. The winged one was huge and hovered about David's neck and shoulders; and the four-legged made circles around the chair, its eyes glowing and its belly low.

Rolling Thunder walked around and around, carrying his medicine fan and contemplating his subject. Again and again he put his mouth on David's neck and shoulders, and there was that high wailing sound that seemed to come from above our heads. With his feathers, he swept the space around and above the seated figure, moving the air like a great wind and making loud whooshing sounds.

When it was over, we moved quickly but quietly back into the house and watched as David was led through the living room to his bed. Rolling Thunder remained outside for his purging. I sat quietly in one of the big chairs to recollect what had happened. I wished to consciously recall what I had seen in the ritual. Only by looking back could I know—in the usual sense of knowing—what I had seen. Only by looking back could I solidly grasp my observations of non-physical phenomena. I needed these quiet moments to mentally imprint my observations before they could be drowned out by the noisy machinery of my intellect. In the moment of the ritual, one can often "see" more than one can "consciously" attend to—so my after-the-fact recollections were needed to induce my brain to assimilate the images that my astral eyes had received. It was like standing in the space between perceiving and pondering—and making the space disappear.

In that space—the space between—another memory of the ritual came to my attention—a recollection of a more substantive phenomenon. It was Rolling Thunder's closing of the ritual. Rolling Thunder, in his usual manner, had closed his healing ritual with a very strong and definite "That's it!" I used to think his "That's it!" sounded something like "Wake up!" But now, in my lucid memory of this evening's ritual, it seemed his words felt more like "Go back to sleep." In the circumstance of the ceremony, one is more awake, I considered, because one can see more. It's like seeing through a wall where one had been using a tiny peephole. Yet, when one looks back afterward, when that awareness is gone, it may be difficult to acknowledge. This closure is important, I thought. It may not be needed for the shaman. The shaman becomes adept at moving between two worlds or extending into both. In any case, every time I'd seen a shaman at work, at least where there had been any number of people present, there had always been a very purposeful and clear closure of the ritual. It is important for those who may have been carried away by the ritual—away from their customary vantage point and away from their culturally-constructed framework of perception. They must come back completely. It is dangerous to be caught midway between two very different perspectives. It is dangerous even to come slowly—or passively—through that midway void. One is vulnerable at such times.

Rolling Thunder remained gone for a long time. Spotted Fawn seemed concerned and twice walked out to where Roll-

170

ing Thunder had been left alone in the bushes far behind his house. "It's hard for him this time," she said to me. "As many times as I've seen him do that, it always does something to me. But this time it's different than I've ever seen it. He's really struggling to purge himself. And it's coming out thick and green from his mouth. I've never seen it like that before."

At last Rolling Thunder came into the house and sat down heavily in the chair beside me. No one spoke. As always, I had no questions and no remarks. It felt best to just sit there. Rolling Thunder was slumped in his chair. It looked strange for him, and I hoped he was recuperating. My thoughts turned to David. I wondered how he was doing. Perhaps Rolling Thunder would check on him later, after he had had a chance to rest.

"Did you get your coffee?" he said abruptly, sitting up in his chair as though he had just come awake.

"No, no, later," I said. But in the pause that followed, Spotted Fawn placed two cups of coffee on the table between us.

"That was death out there," Rolling Thunder said. "That was death. That was a struggle with death himself." He cleared his throat and tried to speak in his usual tone. "But I think David's gonna be all right." He nodded toward the bedroom. "I think he'll be all right, but then, too, it's gonna depend on others." He turned toward me and squinted and pointed his pipestem in the manner that he often used to do when he had something to explain. "David is a spokesman. That's his identity. If a person can't do what he or she's s'posed to do—well, they die. Everybody has to follow his purpose. David is a storyteller, and if a storyteller stops telling stories, he stops having his life. Then he dies.

"These days people have stopped paying attention to the old ones. That's not the way it's s'posed to be. As long as people can keep on doin' what they're s'posed to be doin', they can keep on living. People are s'posed to be supported so they can do their thing. Without the help of others, no people can carry out their identity—I don't care who they are or what they're s'posed to be doin'. And if it doesn't need

171

others, then it's not their true identity—not for this world—
and they might as well not even be here. People keep each
other alive with support. So if someone is a musician, we
ought to listen. If they're a cook, why, you go ahead and eat
and tell 'em how that hit the spot, how you needed that.

"Now, when their time's up and they want to go on, well,
that's a different thing. Then we help 'em and encourage 'em
and let 'em go comfortable. We don't hang on to 'em and try
to hold 'em back. In David's case, he's old, but he's not ready
yet. He knows. He's enough of a medicine man that the man
knows what the spirit wants. Most people don't have that
yet."

Rolling Thunder kept waving his pipe at me. He had come
alive. This thing was important to him and he wanted me to
understand it. This was, in fact, a life-or-death matter with
which he had just been struggling, even at some risk to himself. For a moment I wondered what it was that had to be
neutralized or dissipated in a situation such as David's. This
was more like a social problem. Then I recalled that Rolling
Thunder had called it "death himself."

"How people can be so thoughtless they don't even let a
man carry on his life—" He took a loud sip from his coffee
cup. "How in the world people could have got so much into
their own selves that they don't think they need each other—
I sure can't understand it. If people stop listenin' to David,
now how can he be a storyteller? You tell me. And if he can't
be a storyteller, he'll die. That's the way it works."

◑   ◑   ◑

*In April, 1988, old Grandfather David left his frail and aged
form and moved on. But his prayers will be answered yet.
His stories are alive and his work is in progress. When his
spirit returns, it will have a new form and new stories, but it
will be a storyteller still.*

*I saw David Monongye on several occasions after his heal-
ing at Rolling Thunder's. For several more years he traveled
here and there, lively and energetic, "talking to the people."
Rolling Thunder's steady love and respect helped to keep*

David alive and active for all those later years. People are supposed to be supported, as Rolling Thunder said. "People keep each other alive with support." David had gone around and talked to the people for "a long many years," got "tuckered out," got well again, got up again, and started out all over again. David knew the prophecies—knew what he was looking forward to—for himself and for all life. His vision kept him going, mile after mile, decade after decade. He was a spiritual leader and spokesperson, not only for his Hopi people, but also for all people, for peace, and for the planet. He believed life was returning to the good way—the sacred way. "Everything just goes back to good again," he said, and he kept his heart in his life.

Grandfather David knew when it was time and when he wanted to go on. He knew when he was ready. But Grandfather is always part of the picture, wherever he may be. It is our picture, too. We all have our dynamic and developing designs, but we share the same big picture. The picture has no frame; it simply extends in all directions beyond our conscious view. It is a boundless contexture within whose infinite weavings every living being moves in and out of form—constantly changing places and patterns—and everything keeps going back to good again.

David is enough of a medicine man to know his own spirit. Now he's not "tuckered out" anymore. He can continue. He's gone back to the good way—to the sacred way—but he's a storyteller still. A storyteller keeps coming back. Who will be here when he comes back? What will the people be doing—"brothers and sisters"—when he gets up "to speak again—all over again?" What will the planet be doing? What will life be like? There are the moments of gathering and the moments of telling, and the story never ends. The storyteller continues because life continues—the "things we're looking forward to" and the "things we're supposed to do" continue—and the unfolding story goes on.